The Board Member's Guide

Making a Difference on Your Board and in Your Community

ঌ

Richard Adams
Shirley Magoteaux
Virginia Matz
Cheryl Stiefel-Francis
Judy Westerheide

ঌ

with Donn Vickers

ঌ

Elizabeth Jewell, Editor
Emily Redington, Research

TABLE OF CONTENTS

ACKNOWLEDGEMENTS

Pat Robinson is at the top of the list. She is the one who initially saw the value of this small book and then acted through the Paul G. Duke Foundation to make it possible. She is also the one whose contagious fondness for the people and organizations in Darke, Miami, and Shelby counties inspired us all.

Our advisors have been consistently able and articulate: Jim Daniel, Arthur Haddad, Joanna Hill Heitzman, Sue Parker, Carol Quinter, Sharon Robinson, Ron Scott, Karen Wendeln, and Ken Yowell. They have not only shaped what is here, but already envisioned what will come next. In that regard I wish to personally thank Ken Yowell, President of Edison State Community College, who has hosted our meetings and celebrations and will host in his institution a project that will provide ongoing assistance to the not-for-profit boards in the three counties. Special thanks as well go to Joanna Hill Heitzman and Karen Wendeln, whose careful reading and wise response to drafts greatly improved this publication.

Emily Redington has done just everything it takes to make a publication project like this go well. From research to refreshments, from coordinating meetings to crafting the design and printing, she has been there with competence from beginning to end.

The co-author group of Richard Adams, Shirley Magoteaux, Virginia Matz, Cheryl Stiefel-Francis, and Judy Westerheide has made the doing of this project contain near equal parts of enjoyment and satisfaction. Insofar as these pages address the most important matters in the lives of board members, it is because of them. And insofar as they are addressed well and with clarity, again, they are the ones who get the credit.

With any publication, the last and far from least piece of work is done by an editor. We are all fortunate to have Elizabeth Jewell, someone whose commitment to not-for-profit organizations is matched with her care for making the sentences and paragraphs on these pages smooth and proper. And she, like all those mentioned above, has in so many ways made this book project an experience full of good and long-lasting memories.

Donn F. Vickers
January 1, 2003

FOREWARD

Communities characterized by quality are not the result of good luck nor do they occur accidentally. Outstanding communities are created and maintained by a number of factors. Among the most important factors are dedicated not-for-profit board members who perform their duties with enthusiasm and competence.

Community residents usually recognize and appreciate their quality of life. Many of them realize that an important component of the quality is the number of persons who serve on the many volunteer boards within their community.

Perhaps the perspective of many citizens in this particular three-county area would best be described by the idea that "if better is possible... good is not enough." It is with this notion that a group of six co-authors, with the assistance of an advisory committee, made the commitment to prepare this resource for not-for-profit boards and individual board members.

The people who have worked on this effort are hopeful that boards and board members will consider this book to be useful and a source of motivation. With these goals in mind the co-authors will be working with officials at Edison Community College to establish a center for preparing new board members, in addition to providing appropriate seminars for experienced board members who desire to improve their abilities.

The not-for-profit board and the individual board members are vitally important to the success of the organizations they lead. Good organizations have good leaders. Outstanding organizations have outstanding leaders. As board members serve they recognize the satisfaction received from that service. Frequently this experience results in even more service and more satisfaction. We anticipate this book will provide readers with many ideas to help them do a good, or, better yet, an outstanding job of serving.

The co-authors express appreciation to the Paul G. Duke Foundation for the idea of this project, encouragement, and funding which resulted in this book. Gratitude is also cited for the expertise and technical assistance provided by the staff of the Academy for Leadership and Governance.

Richard N. Adams, Ph.D.
January 1, 2003

Section I

The Individual and the Board

Chapter 1

Satisfactions

You might have guessed we would start with service. It's a good word and one most of us think about when getting involved with a committee at school, as a volunteer at the hospital, or on the board at the United Way or the arts council.

Another good word is satisfaction. When organizations were first created in our communities to deal with health, music, the environment, young children, senior citizens, or people who are hungry or homeless, it usually was an attempt to make life more satisfying: both for the members of our communities and for ourselves. Health care does that as does education, music, gardens, and of course a decent place to live and food to eat. By being involved in the not-for-profit community, we are all in the life-satisfaction business. In a variety of ways we are working to make life more satisfying for the people in our communities.

We believe that everything goes better if those of us who are doing this work are having a personally satisfying experience most of the time. Getting satisfaction out of giving satisfaction is a worthy goal.

A not-so-good way to participate is to have too many of the people on any given board having an unsatisfying experience too much of the time. Here are two ideas about how to avoid dissatisfaction in pursuit of good in your community.

1. Make sure you understand and care deeply about the mission of the organization. All social service organizations, as well as those that deal with health, education, or the arts need board members who understand finance, marketing, volunteerism, event planning, and working with committees. But more than anything else they need people who are passionate about their mission—people who love kids, or dance, or wildlife, or scouting. That's the first and most important match. That is the beginning of satisfaction—

being involved in something about which you care deeply. When you do that, you are doing a big favor to the organization and those whom it serves, and you will be happier yourself.

2. Make sure that how you are involved both builds on some things you know and causes you to learn some new things. If you are a secretary in your work life, you just may not want to be a secretary for the board—that job you know too well. If you own your own small business and spend a lot of time trying to make the books balance, you may not want to chair the finance committee. Do something new and fresh that will help you grow. We have found that most people in their volunteer lives want a break from what they do otherwise, and most people volunteer at least partly to learn something new.

REFLECTING ON MOTIVES

There are a variety of reasons that people join organizations and get involved on boards. Some of the reasons are more related to one's self-interest and some more related to the generous desire to serve. There is seldom a single reason that people get involved. Usually, it is a mix of two, three, or more. Think about this for yourself and think about it as you try to engage others. The chart that follows lists motives for participation that we have found in our work with boards and organizations. First, read them over and see which two or three most apply to you. And then, if these are the major reasons that you get involved, decide whether it is working out as you had hoped. Finally, consider what you can do to see that you get more of what you had hoped for in the first place.

You may want to ask your fellow board members to read over the list. Ask them if there are any additional motives. Are all of these motives good reasons to participate or are there some we don't like? What are the advantages and disadvantages of having board members who have a different set of motives?

Then have your board members check the top two or three reasons that they themselves have for participating. Copy out the form and use it with our good wishes. Talk about those results and what it means for your board. What, if anything, does it say about the kind of people you should be recruiting?

The goal here is to get a clearer picture about why people participate so that more of them will have a satisfying experience more of the time. Go about this exercise with a thoughtfulness that does not slip into too much seriousness.

Motives for Board Participation

Motive	Relative influence Highest = 5, Lowest = 1				
	5	4	3	2	1
Commitment to cause	❏	❏	❏	❏	❏
Affiliation need	❏	❏	❏	❏	❏
Political aspirations	❏	❏	❏	❏	❏
Utilization of talent	❏	❏	❏	❏	❏
Learning and self-improvement	❏	❏	❏	❏	❏
Civic responsibility	❏	❏	❏	❏	❏
Business contacts	❏	❏	❏	❏	❏
Public visibility	❏	❏	❏	❏	❏
Personal/social contacts	❏	❏	❏	❏	❏
Development of hobby or interest	❏	❏	❏	❏	❏
Status	❏	❏	❏	❏	❏
Career enhancement	❏	❏	❏	❏	❏
Other: _____	❏	❏	❏	❏	❏
Other: _____	❏	❏	❏	❏	❏
Other: _____	❏	❏	❏	❏	❏

Chapter 2

Recruiting and Selecting
Board Members

This chapter focuses on you as an individual board member and on other individuals in your town or neighborhood who ought to be serving with you. We believe that the business of recruitment and selection of board members may be one of the most important things you do in the life of your organization. However, our experience is that all too often recruitment is too much a last-minute task accomplished with too little planning. Therefore, our first big message is: take time, get organized, and use your best imagination and contacts to put together a top-notch, diverse, and enthused group of potential board members.

Start with designating a three- or four-member **nominating committee.** Pick as members those individuals who seem to know the most people and those who will be willing to devote ten or twelve months a year to this important task rather than just one or two. This extended time will allow for careful and broad thought about new potential candidates. In too many towns, a small number of all the same people serve on most of the boards. That is usually because the recruitment procedure goes something like this: "Well, it's November again. Do you know anyone who might like to be on our board?" That narrow, last minute process is sure to produce a board of known neighbors and colleagues who may or may not care about your mission and will pretty much look like every other board in town. Finding people who can care about your mission involves much searching, asking, and checking that should take months, not weeks. No doubt, hidden in neighborhoods, work places, social clubs, and service organizations are people who may be wild about nutrition or seniors or dance or any number of different missions. They can be found. Often your local community leadership program or United Way can be of help. Wherever they come from, those new faces who care greatly about your mission are important because they can challenge and re-enliven trusted board veterans.

Occasionally, you may have a nominating committee without total control over its recommendations. If your by-laws provide for the board to elect its own members or for the membership to choose board members, the nominating committee can be a major influence. Where board members are elected by the general public or selected by an outside appointing authority, suggestions are in order but influence is often limited. In either case, exercise all the influence you can in understanding the board's membership needs and finding the best people to fill those positions.

Make sure you pursue various constituents when selecting new members. Also, don't forget to consider those who already volunteer or serve on committees. Many people other than board members have a stake in your organization, including funders, government officials, community leaders, past board members, and past and present clients. Along with their interest comes a perception about the board, its composition, and effectiveness. Their sense of the kind of people your board should be recruiting is important. By soliciting suggestions from these sources, you develop new networks, broaden your perspective, and extend your reach into the community.

What follows are guidelines, processes, and forms that you can use as you sit with and instruct the nominating committee about its work. Feel free to make copies and decide together what and how you can make best use of them in your situation.

LOOKING AT YOUR PRESENT BOARD: SKILLS, SECTORS, AND DEMOGRAPHICS

A good place to start is looking squarely at the make-up of your present board. We suggest three ways of doing this assessment: by skills (what abilities do they have), by sectors (what parts of the community do they represent), and by demographics (age, gender, and ethnicity).

Let's start with **skills**. Here, as with the areas of sectors and demographics, the main issue is diversity. All boards need financial people but not only financial people. Also, don't get caught believing that having Skill A means having a career in Skill A. Many people have abilities based on previous volunteer or life experiences. It is the ability we are seeking, regardless of the way it was developed.

The board skills chart follows. Review the skill areas and add additional ones to fit your situation. Then mark each area with the number of board members who have that skill. Remember it is not unusual for one board member to bring two or more skills. Now compile all the check marks (it may be useful—even fun and creative—to do this with your board) and look at where you are strong and where you need to add strength. Decide which areas are most important to add for the upcoming year.

Board Skills Inventory

Skill	Present board members' strengths	Skill areas we wish to add or supplement
Programming		
Event planning		
Finance		
Fundraising		
Personnel		
Public relations		
Legal matters		
Building and grounds		
Long-range planning		
Board development		
Volunteerism		
Other: _____		

Now let's look at **community sectors.** Our experience is that boards are stronger and better able to serve the community if they are broadly representative of the community in which they wish to do their work. Another chart follows. Make sure all your key community sectors are represented. If you are sitting with your board, have them each check areas that they represent (sometimes more than one). Compile the individual lists and see what is missing. Then decide how important that missing sector is for your organization at this time.

Profile of Board Community Sectors

Sector	Number of present board members	Sector areas to consider this year
Business		
Professional		
Government		
Union		
Volunteer		
Clients or customers		
Arts and culture		
Education		
Agriculture		
Other: _____		

Finally, consider **demographics.** This one is likely to require a little conversation. For instance, we have discovered that while younger people may lack some experience, they often bring a unique and necessary perspective, as they represent the future of the community. Regarding race and ethnicity, it is best to know your area and see that it is represented fairly on your board. If there are no citizens in your town who are Native Americans, it would be artificial (perhaps impossible) to recruit a Native American board member. The chart is to help you assess who you have and who you wish to recruit.

Profile of Board Demographics		
Criteria	Number of board members in each category	Board members you wish to recruit
AGE		
Youth		
20 – 35		
36 – 50		
51 – 64		
65 or over		
SEX		
Male		
Female		
RACE/ETHNICITY		
African-American		
Asian-American		
Latino/Latina		
Native American		
Caucasian		
Other		
RESIDENCE		
Center city		
City neighborhood		
Suburban area		
Rural area		

Some final questions

All qualities important to board membership cannot be captured in a single profile. There are additional questions worth considering and sometimes asking of potential board members. The following have been useful to a variety of boards:

1. How has the person demonstrated a serious interest in our mission?

2. What is the person's potential for board leadership?

3. Is the person available only for consultation?

4. Is the person available for planning and development?

5. Is the person available for committee work?

6. Does the person represent a client group of the organization, and therefore a possible conflict of interest?

7. Can the person be an effective link to important constituent groups?

8. Is this someone with whom you will enjoy working?

Some key things to communicate to the candidates

During board member recruitment, you will want to be sending messages about your organization's history, vision, and present challenges. Make sure you receive information as well. Recruitment is less a sales pitch and more the establishment of a relationship with a new neighbor. That means you need to listen for common interests and shared values that match the essence of what your organization is about. An individual's demographics and skills may fit well with your profile, but remember, you are looking for someone who has a special personal connection to the central purpose of your organization.

On the sending messages side, complaints often heard from new board members include that it was not made clear how much time would be involved or what would be the responsibility for financial contributions. Be up front and clear about the twin powerhouses of time and money. Consider these sample questions that you should be prepared to answer for potential board members.

- How many board meetings do you hold a year?

- What are the expectations for attendance?

- How much time is allotted for each meeting?

- What is the expectation for committee service and attendance at organizational functions?

- What else is expected of all board members?

- Is there an expected financial contribution?

- Do board members have liability exposure?

When recruiting board members and telling your story, be sure everyone is telling the same story and the whole story.

One more note on financial expectations: most boards find it useful in fundraising if they can state that all board members contribute financially to the organization. Some set a standard for giving for all and others believe that there are a variety of ways to give, and that money is but one, professional service time being another. Problems most often occur when board members discover the money rules after getting on the board. Whatever your financial expectations or requirements are (and they may need discussing), state them in advance.

As you can see, recruiting board members takes some time. We conclude, though, that it is time well spent. Finding those individuals whose passion and abilities fit your board and selecting people of diverse backgrounds is what makes our community boards strong, connected, and productive.

In conclusion, we suggest you use the dozen questions that follow when considering board membership or approaching other prospective board members.

A dozen smart questions to ask before you say yes to a board (or someone else says yes to your board)

1. What does your organization do that makes you enthused about being part of it?

2. Who in our community most benefits from the work your organization does?

3. Besides money, what are the two or three biggest challenges your organization faces in this upcoming year?

4. What do you believe to be the strengths and weaknesses of your executive?

5. What are the strengths and weaknesses of your board?

6. What are the terms of office for board members?

7. How many board meetings a year are there and how long is each one?

8. How many hours on top of board meetings do most board members spend working with the organization?

9. What are the organization's funding sources?

10. How did you end the year last year financially? Is there a rainy day fund or endowment?

11. What is expected of board members in terms of giving and getting?

12. Do you have liability insurance? Have you determined that you need it?

Chapter 3

Preparing and Developing
Board Members

Because you read the previous chapter and decided to put it into practice, you have recruited and selected really good board members. Right? Our experience is that if you didn't, it will take far more than this chapter can give to make your new recruits work well. Preparing and developing *carefully selected* board members is another matter. It takes some thoughtful time and effort, but it all pays off and, in the end, is greatly rewarding.

The first step is preparing new board members, often called orientation. We'll suggest a few things to avoid and then provide a detailed outline for a session or two on orientation. The second step is nurturing the ongoing development of board members. That development is best done with a good deal of reflection and evaluation. We'll offer three different ways for board members to assess their work and decide what they need to do better or differently.

ORIENTATION

Some boards have board member orientation conducted by a personnel or board development committee. Other boards appoint a seasoned board member to a one-on-one mentoring role with incoming members. Sometimes the executive director has a partial responsibility in orienting new members to the board. You need to decide what works best for your situation. Whatever it may be, what follows is a one-page outline for an orientation conversation with new board members. Note that the first half is focused on asking and listening. That's always an effective way to begin any learning experience. In this case it also communicates respect for the experiences of the new recruits.

OUTLINE FOR ORIENTATION CONVERSATION

New board members

1. Things to listen for: Learning something new from the recruit

- What is the new member's view, as a relative outsider, of your organization's special role in the community?

- What does the new member perceive to be the unique character/culture of the organization that needs to be preserved and nourished?

- Which activities of your organization does she see as vital to your community?

- What aspects of your organization seem to him to be less well developed and in need of strengthening?

- What confuses or weakens your image in the community?

- For what in the organization does the new recruit want to take some responsibility?

2. Things to say: Deciding how to briefly say what is most important

- What the initial need, spark, or enthusiasm was that got your organization going.

- How that initial focus has developed and changed.

- What the three or four most important challenges are in the next 12 to 24 months.

- What about your organization worries you most.

- In what areas the organization needs help or new leadership.

- Information concerning finance, other board and committee members, contributors, meeting times and dates, by-laws, and reporting requirements, in addition to other basic organizational information.

3. **What unanswered questions remain?**

4. **How might the orientation have been more effective?**

Over the years we've made some mistakes and learned what not to do during board member orientation. Here's a summary of that experience in three Don'ts.

1. **Don't skip the orientation because the new board members seem smart enough without it.**

Doing so communicates a lack of seriousness about the work of the board ("anybody can do this without thinking about it"). Even very smart people may still lack information and perspective on your particular board's priorities, key challenges, and financial state.

2. **Don't assume that everyone is so busy that you can orient a half-hour before the first board meeting.**

This is a sure way to communicate again that the orientation process is unimportant. It will feel harried and hurried as executive and board president slip into board meeting anxiety. Orientation is worth at least an hour to an hour and one-half, and worth a quiet, separate time that says "we believe this work is important enough to warrant ample preparation."

3. **Don't overload with paper and details.**

An orientation that consists primarily in handing out by-laws, minutes, strategic plans, budgets, and rosters is better done by mail. Rather, this should be a time of helping the new board member understand the three to five most crucial goals for the year and the two to four bigger problems or challenges the organization faces. That takes thoughtful conversation and questions. Most of the really important documents can be distributed in five to ten minutes.

ONGOING DEVELOPMENT
AND EVALUATION

First you may be asking, "Whose job is board development and evaluation?" Sometimes there is a small board development committee that pays attention to the new information and issues the board needs to know. Sometimes the personnel committee expands to attend to the board as "personnel." Sometimes either the board president or the executive or both will fill this function. You decide, but do decide and lodge the task with someone who—perhaps one to four times a year as part of the board meeting—will prepare a time for board development.

Next you might wonder, what issues should we be addressing? We find it helpful to think of two kinds: those that are part of the social and political environment that affect the organization, and those that relate to how we function together as a board and as individual members of the board. An example of the first issue would be changes in the tax laws on charitable giving or governmental policy changes that affect how the organization is regulated or funded. An example of the second issue might include board committee structure, roles of board and staff, or the functions of the executive committee. The following methods aim to address those issues in three ways. Keep in mind that the chief reason for the board to assess its work is so that it might do it better.

1. Review the work of the board.

The full range of all that a board does is really very impressive. This method centers on a few major and common tasks on the agenda of most boards. The purpose is not to assign a rank to "how we did in each." Instead, review all the items as a reminder of the breadth of activity and select three or four to concentrate on for the coming six months to a year. Specify what "concentrate on" means. What more or different do you want to do about item two or item seven? Who will be responsible to see that it gets done? In short, the full board should decide on the items, suggest goals pertaining to the mission, establish who will be responsible, and identify a time to review the progress. The checklist that follows is not the entire catalogue of board tasks and responsibilities, but it does encompass enough of the major ones for your board to settle on three or four that need concentrated attention.

Checklist of potential board tasks

❏ Establish orientation procedures for new board members.

❏ Develop a way to create effective agendas for board meetings.

❏ Create a process for assisting the board to learn about current issues related to your organization's mission.

❏ Ensure that there is balance between the detail work of committees and big issues work at board meetings.

❏ Explore ways of making more appropriate committee assignments and rotating committee chairs and members.

❏ Design an organizational planning process and a way to plan revision.

❏ Improve the developing and monitoring of the budgetary process.

❏ Enlarge the base of revenue support for the organization.

❏ Review the number and duration of board and committee meetings.

❏ Evaluate and encourage the executive.

❏ Forecast and prepare a succession plan for the executive's replacement.

❏ Recommend changes in the way key decisions are made within the organization.

❏ Re-evaluate core programs and services.

❏ Propose new strategies for marketing and public relations.

❏ Examine the sufficiency of existing personnel policies and procedures.

❏ Expand participation and collaboration with other organizations in your community.

2. Survey board member participation.

This method may work best in the form of an outline completed by individual board members and then discussed individually with the board president or chair of the nominating committee. The goal is to assist board members not only in becoming more involved, but also in becoming more appropriately involved. These questions—either sent out to board members or used as part of a reflective time at a board meeting (with responses collected on the spot)—may assist you in better utilizing the resources of your board membership.

Inventory of Board Member Participation

1. In the upcoming year on the board I would like to take personal responsibility for _____.

2. I would be willing to have further conversation about being considered for the following offices and committee chair positions: President, Vice President, Secretary, Treasurer, (list your committees)

3. My previous board involvement has been mostly _____. I would like to move toward _____.

4. A new effort I think is important for our organization and that I would like to help with is _____.

5. A task I particularly enjoy at work or home that I have yet to do on this board is _____.

6. My most treasured board experience has had to do with _____.

7. I would consider this upcoming year a success if the board was able to _____.

---

3. Have board members set personal goals

In most organizations the executive together with the board establishes some personal goals for the work of the executive in the new year. Sometimes that same practice would be useful for board members as well. We suggest two guidelines when asking board members to consider setting their own goals: simplicity (not too many) and flexibility (choices). What follows is one outline to assist board members in their own personal goal setting. We recommend that each board member fill it out individually, and then share it with the board president for review at year's end.

Board Member Personal Goal Setting

Name_____

For the time period _____ to _____

Note: Please select and fill in at least _____ goals.

1. My personal goal for board meeting attendance is _____.

2. Over the year my goal is to give an additional ___ hours a month on average.

3. Through the annual fund and various fund-raising events I plan to donate _____.

4. The one thing for which I will take leadership is _____.

5. I will represent this organization by attendance and/or speaking at the following event(s): _____.

6. I will take an active part on the following board committee(s): _____.

7. I plan to educate myself about one aspect of this organization about which I am not well informed. That would be _____.

8. I will introduce _____ new prospective volunteers to the organization.

9. I will personally invite and host _____ guests to organizational events as follows: _____.

10. I will seek to assist the executive and/or board president in the following special way: _____.

Chapter 4

Volunteers Work

Here's a sentiment that we particularly dislike: "If you expect to get that done you'll have to pay somebody. You just can't trust volunteers." Unfortunately, we have heard these words more than a few times. The problem is that if it were really true, we'd have to shut down about half of the not-for-profit organizations in our towns and communities. Our sector is, by definition, volunteer-dependent and proud of it. Some who write about the group of organizations in which we serve even refer to us as the "voluntary sector." What that means is that we participate in the life of these organizations because we choose to do so freely. And in this case freely means both freely, without monetary compensation, and freely as in by our own choosing. Money is not the issue and money is not what makes us work hard.

When you think about it, we all know people who work for pay who don't get the job done well—who don't follow through. Pay does not guarantee commitment or completion. Overall, really good people do well at jobs, and while some of those really good people are paid for that effort, some are volunteers. Therefore, we deeply believe in the title of this chapter, "Volunteers Work." They do work and it is a very good thing because so many of our organizations just could not exist without them. What we wish to do here is share our experience about how volunteers can work well and how they too can have a satisfying experience in our organizations.

We have organized our own experience about volunteers into four sections: thinking about what you need, getting the word out, placing and preparing with care, and attending and recognizing. While much of this is just good common sense about dealing with people, we hope you'll find a new idea or two that will make for happier volunteers and a stronger organization.

1. Thinking about what you need

To say "we need volunteers" is to say everything and nothing. People tend not to simply say, "Sure, I'd like to volunteer." They are more apt to say, "I'd be willing to help with events or organizing the files." And so our first word about this is specify, specify, specify. Take time with your board (and maybe existing volunteers) to think through all that needs to get done on a week-in, week-out basis and what of that you would want for volunteers to do.

Start by making a list. Our guess is that you can come up with ten or twelve specific items. That's important because you will then be able to expand what it is that volunteers can do (versus board or staff) and it will be far easier to find people with a detailed list because they then have some idea what it is they are being asked to do. We tried a list, actually made a one-page form out of it, and then tried to make it a bit fun. See what you think.

Ten Terrific Opportunities to Volunteer at The Center for Young Children

Note: Check as many as appeal to you. Indicate your availability and give us your name and phone. We promise to call back within three days and schedule a personal conversation within ten.

- ❏ True, I like to get mail but I don't mind sending it. I'll help out with mailings.

- ❏ Telephones are friendlier than e-mail. I'll be glad to be a telephone receptionist.

- ❏ Organized, I am. Let me at those files or that supplies cabinet.

- ❏ I not only like parties, I like organizing them. I'd enjoy planning events.

- ❏ I never wrote a novel but I like writing and would be happy to help with press releases or articles for the local paper.

- ❏ I balance the family checkbook and actually enjoy it. I'd be glad to help with financial records and reports.

- ❏ It's been 17 years since I took typing in high school, but I can word process meeting minutes, letters, or articles.

- ❏ I love history and would be glad to organize all the pictures, papers, articles, and records from the beginning of the organization.

- ❏ Setting up meetings takes time but since I like talking on the phone, let me do it.

- ❏ I know how important "thank you" is and I'd be glad to send thank you notes out regularly to those who give their time or money.

Speaking of time, I can give about _____ hours a week/month (circle one). The best time of day for me is _____ to _____.

My name is _____.

You may reach me at _____.

2. Getting the word out

Whether you use the form on the previous page or one that you adopt for your own organization, you now have a clear word to get out, which is a great start. Why not begin the process by placing copies in every library, church, and friendly grocery store and doctor's office you frequent? Make it bright yellow and we will almost guarantee that you'll get responses. Remember to think of this as a gift you are giving. Nothing is more important to people than the opportunity to do good work that is personally satisfying. For many, they do not have that experience where they work. No doubt you yourself have experienced how much meaning and reward your own volunteering has brought to you.

Here are two other quick ideas about "getting the word out" that we have seen work. Take 15 minutes at your next board meeting and ask everyone to think of neighbors, people at work, or people from their church or service club who might enjoy being part of your organization. Maybe offer a small prize for the best recruiter. Surely each board member could come up with two or three names to whom they could personally give your bright yellow form.

Secondly, think about having an annual volunteer fair in your community. Organize it with two or three other organizations or with your chamber or leadership program. Spend Saturday morning at the mall or courthouse or library or your own community's favorite Saturday morning gathering place, handing out information and your bright yellow form.

3. Choosing and preparing carefully

Amazingly, we are bold enough to say that not everyone has a perfect sense of what he can do well, so you may have to help a prospective volunteer get in the right place. It is important to remember that volunteers can be effective in their work and have a satisfying experience at the same time. After talking you may suggest that they try item 3 on the form, not item 7. The fact is that from experience you know better what is required in a certain area and therefore can be helpful to them in making the best choice. "Try it" is the phrase to keep in mind. They are not signing up for life. The potential volunteer should probably try out the task or committee for two or three months to see if it works for both them and you.

Assume that the new volunteer will want to do a good job and will be happy to have your help in preparing to do so. Make sure all the necessary information is provided and that they know both the purpose of the project, as well as how you like to have it done. This will take some time, but this little bit of advice and preparation up front can make a big difference. It says to the new volunteer that you care a lot about the importance of this work.

4. Recognition

If you've done a good job specifying your volunteer opportunities and taken the time to know, place, and prepare your volunteers, then the recognition part is easy. Now you can mostly be aware of all the good people helping out in one way or another, talk to them about how it is going, and let them know how much you appreciate their work. You may want to have an annual volunteer recognition dessert, tea, or dinner. You may want to have certificates or special pin-on nametags. There are a variety of ways to show that you recognize them and are grateful for the work they do.

If you are able to help people to do what they like and to realize that the contributions they are making are valuable, that is often reward enough.

The key to a successful volunteer program is having volunteers do something they enjoy where they feel they are making a meaningful contribution in an amount of time that fits nicely into their lives. The amount of time part is crucial: you don't want stressed or exhausted volunteers, because they go away. You want happy campers—people who will stay with you and be helpful over the years. Sometimes you may even need to help protect them against doing too much. You'll have to decide when and how to do that, but do it if you must. They will feel better about their work and stay longer, which of course benefits everyone.

Section II
The Work of the Board

Chapter 5

The Mission Statement

The first question may be, "Does anyone know where the mission statement is?" Too often it is in a file, in the minutes, or otherwise fairly hidden. We have also experienced two other problems with mission statements. Some were written twenty-three years ago and no longer represent the scope of what the organization does. The statement worked well in the beginning with five board members, a half-time executive, and a budget of $35,000. Now with four times the budget, two and one-half staff, and five different program areas, the 1980's mission statement doesn't work.

The second problem may be that the mission statement, however old, is totally uninspiring and not memorable. That's too bad, because at one time, when the organization was initiated, people presumably had to care passionately enough about its mission to go to the trouble of founding it. That kind of passion should have been captured in words and stated and framed as a strong statement of mission. Oftentimes it was not.

So what to do? Let's say you find the mission statement and it's just okay—a little limited, maybe, and a little lacking in fire. We suggest you grapple with the main purpose you have, respect the wishes of the founders, and try new language that works for your situation now in this twenty-first century reality. Why? Well, the process of struggling with the mission statement as a board can be a useful experience in learning and finding direction. It is also crucial to have an agreed-upon statement by which to guide the program decisions of your organization. In short, a good mission statement is worth framing because it can inspire and focus the energies of your board as they direct the organization.

Here are some examples, followed by a short guide to re-writing your mission statement. First, the not-so-good mission statement:

Theaterworks was founded so that people of all ages could experience drama and know its value as a form of art that has existed for hundreds of years and has been appreciated by all generations.

What's the problem? Or rather, what are the problems?

1. It is dull. Where is the passion?
2. It is vague. Do they produce plays, go to plays, or what?
3. It is past tense.

Try this for contrast:

Theaterworks produces plays from three continents for teenage youth in support of our belief in diversity of artistic expression.

What's better?

1. It is concise.
2. It is specific about what the organization does.
3. It is clear about its audience.
4. It expresses a strong value.

Here are some steps to change your own mission statement from not-so-good to much better:

STEP 1 Get your whole board involved for 30 to 45 minutes at each of two meetings. Conversations like this take time and are better done over a period of weeks or months.

STEP 2 Have a conversation. What is the key set of values and beliefs that we wish to have form all that we do? Make sure you can say it in one sentence that contains some of that initial energy or fire.

STEP 3 Have another conversation. What specifically do we want to do in programs and services that grows out of those values. This may be a short list of things in a sentence without the details of dates, times, or numbers.

STEP 4 Have one more conversation. Who is our primary audience, the people we most want to serve? Don't say how or when—that's planning.

STEP 5 Visualize it all as follows and discuss how it looks and sounds.

STEP 6 Write it out in short paragraph form in as lively and inspiring a way as you can.

STEP 7 Let it sit. Come back to it and revise after sharing it with others, including donors and past board members.

Developing a mission statement is worth the time and effort. It will likely be a good learning experience that ends up producing a mission statement worthy of a frame rather than a file.

Chapter 6

Getting Organized

Too much of what we have read about boards and board leadership stresses the way everyone "ought to" organize and function. It is as though somewhere out there is the perfect pattern or mold that we all should copy. The fact is there are very few things that you absolutely *must* do as a board, and a very great number that you can invent for your particular situation and the special people who serve with you in the positions of leadership. We greatly favor putting you and your fellow board members in charge of determining the "what works best for us" question, rather than urging you to follow the dictates of some rulebook.

We think the most exciting part of being on a board is the many choices available to create and recreate the kind of board and organization you wish to have. You can have a board of five or fifty. You can meet twelve times a year or three. You can have all the staff sit in on your meetings or none but the executive. You can have board members sit in on staff meetings or have no interaction with staff. You can even start every meeting with a reading from an article that pertains to your work, or end every meeting with good news reports about your programs. The point is that you can and should take hold of the personality of the place—the way things are done, the way decisions are made, the way people are treated—and with your colleagues create a distinctive setting that gives a special organizational character to all you do.

In what follows there is a distinct absence of "always" and "never." Except in matters of truth and theft, words like always and never have little place in organizational life. The precise set of skills board members must always have, what community sectors board members should always represent, what roles—paid or unpaid—leaders should never perform seem to us less and less clear the more we are acquainted with the rich and complex variety of organizations in the not-for-profit sector. If someone asks if a board member should be involved in programming or if an executive should assist with investment policy, the answer must certainly be "it depends." It depends on the people but most importantly it depends on the kind of organization you wish to have.

Let's start with a brief word about numbers of board members and numbers of meetings. As we said, there are no rules about how many board members you should have. The number you have may be just right. If it feels like it isn't, it is easy to change, often without even changing the by-laws. Many times the by-laws will indicate a minimum or maximum number, such as "up to eighteen." Our own experience is that eighteen can be right but so can nine. Having fewer than nine can make it difficult to accomplish all the work, and having more than eighteen presents a management challenge. You'll note that all the numbers we have suggested are multiples of three. That way you can have three classes of board members with no more than one-third of the board completing their term of service at a time.

Another decision you need to make is about meetings. More often these busy days we find boards meeting four or six times a year. Most by-laws are written to permit a flexibility in number of meetings. Board members need time to work on committees and prefer not to spend so much of their valuable time in board meetings. If you were to change from ten or twelve meetings to six you may decide to have some communication to update the board on the months they are not meeting. You may want to consider e-mail for this purpose. We find that people quickly get in the pattern of attending fewer meetings, like it, and make those meetings far more full and productive. Try a change, maybe for a year, and then evaluate. Again, no one can say what works best in all towns or in all organizations.

STRUCTURING THE WORK OF THE BOARD

For ease of comparison we selected two boards of about the same size—fifteen and eighteen members—with budgets in the $100,000 to $300,000 range, and both roughly in the business of providing human services. We do believe that regardless of your mission, one of these two models, or a combination of them, will work just fine when considering how to structure the work of the board.

1. Advance Unlimited

Advance Unlimited is an organization that supports teenage youth who are unlikely to go on to higher education due to financial and/or family difficulties, but who may be more likely to succeed given timely advice and financial support. The chart on the next page outlines how they have structured their work.

Type of meetings	Number of annual sessions	Board person involved	Staff person involved
Board	10 yearly	President	Executive
Exec. Committee	6 yearly	President	Executive
Program	10 yearly	Vice President	Part-time Program Director
Finance	10 yearly	Treasurer	Executive
Fund Development	6 yearly	President	Executive
Facilities	4 yearly	Board member	Administrative Asst.
Planning & Eval.	6 yearly	Vice President	Executive
Personnel	3 yearly	Board Member	n/a
Marketing & PR	6 yearly	Secretary	Part-time Marketing Director

Of course, some things are not easily accommodated by the above chart. The executive committee is comprised of the four officers (President, Vice President, Secretary, and Treasurer) plus the board chairs of each of the committees. The executive committee is careful not to do business which is then repeated at the board meeting. Its function is to review the progress of the committees and in so doing, develop a plan for the board meeting.

Note that the board president is fairly intimately involved in three areas: the board, the executive committee, and the committee on fund development. Note also that staff people meet with committees that are related to the work they do. Only the executive attends the meetings of the board and executive committee. This model is fairly standard but also very workable.

Now you can use the blank chart on the next page (remember, feel free to make copies) to have a discussion about how your board currently functions and about how you might like to change.

Type of meeting	Number of annual sessions	Board member involved	Staff involved

2. Transitions for Women

Transitions for Women does its work primarily with women who are in the process of making educational and career decisions. Like Advance Unlimited, they have been in existence for over twenty years and are in reasonably good financial shape. The chart that follows outlines a different way of structuring work.

Type of meetings	Number of meetings	Board officer	Staff involved
Board	4 yearly	President	Executive
Exec. Committee	3 yearly	President	Executive
Education Programs	6 yearly	Board Member	Director of Education
Counseling Programs	6 yearly	Board Member	Director of Counseling
Finance & Funding	6 yearly	Treasurer	Financial Officer
Board Development	6 yearly	Vice President	Executive
Human Resources	6 yearly	Board Member	Executive
Outreach & PR	6 yearly	Board Member	Assistant Director

This way of structuring the work of the board is not better or worse, only different. There are far fewer board and executive meetings, which forces more of the work into committees. The important function of planning and evaluation is no longer in a specific committee, but carried out by the executive committee. There are two major aspects of programming, each assigned to a separate committee. A new committee, board development, is charged with enhancing the abilities of board members. Finally, there is a human resources committee which is charged with the traditional personnel functions, as well as staff development and the recruitment and training of volunteers.

You might choose to use either of these charts as the basis for a discussion on what aspects of them you might want to incorporate into your organization's way of working.

Reviewing your board's involvement in organizational tasks

One more chart that might be the basis for good board discussion focuses on eight essential board tasks that are fairly unavoidable. Take the opportunity to think through these tasks and identify which individuals or committees might share in them.

Decide which program and administrative functions you wish to review. You may want to begin by indicating the way things are and then redo the form according to the ideal for your organization. It is likely that neither the board nor the executive always formulates or always implements. You are looking for the predominant pattern, the way it most often works. Equally important, you are looking for the way you want it to be in the future.

Board Involvement Review

Organizational function	Board President	Board	Executive Committee	Specific Committee	Executive
Create/initiate	❑	❑	❑	❑	❑
Formulate/conceptualize	❑	❑	❑	❑	❑
Propose/present	❑	❑	❑	❑	❑
Decide/approve	❑	❑	❑	❑	❑
Implement/execute	❑	❑	❑	❑	❑
Monitor/manage	❑	❑	❑	❑	❑
Assess/evaluate	❑	❑	❑	❑	❑
Reformulate/refine	❑	❑	❑	❑	❑

We believe it preferable to discuss your observations with the executive in preparation for a lively conversation with your full board. Remember: all this is about creating structures and patterns for working that engage board members and are more likely to get the work done effectively and efficiently.

Chapter 7

Planning

The need to plan may sneak up on you in a variety of ways. As you are reading the new funding guidelines for your local United Way, arts agency, or community foundation, you might run into the boldface type, "Every organization requesting funds must provide a three-year strategic plan." Or it could just be that your organization has a history of writing a plan every three years and though it seems only months since the last planning process ended, it truly is time to begin again.

The reason for "doing a plan" may also come from a budget crisis, personnel problem, split in the board, or just general dissatisfaction about how things are going. On the other hand, planning can be a positive, invigorating, even inspiring thing to do. For whatever reason it presents itself, planning is largely unavoidable, often surprisingly useful, and usually able to be accomplished successfully without a three-day retreat, a high-priced consultant, or an exhausted board.

Let's look at some basic questions for you to explore as you bring your full board to a thoughtful planning process that works for your organization. First, consider who should be involved. For some it will be consumers or clients, and for others, major funders, government agencies, or appointing authorities. You might consider potential (or actual) collaborators, representatives of parallel agencies in other communities, faculty and researchers, media representatives, and specific ethnic groups presently under-represented in your organization. Involving outsiders often is not a neat, tidy, or comfortable experience. It may, however, be the most effective way for you to develop a good plan.

IS THERE SUCH A THING
AS A GOOD TIME TO PLAN?

There is probably no perfect time to initiate a planning process, rather the question is one of readiness. When are you most likely to get the best attention of the people you want to have participate? The following list presents planning times some organizations have determined to be right:

- Just before a new fiscal year. Budgetary decisions are made at this time and it may also be the opportune moment to ask about broader organizational issues.

- When you are about to select a new executive director or new board members. In either case leadership selection decisions can be better informed if they are influenced by a thoughtful organizational planning process.

- At the time you install new officers or a new executive director. A time of leadership change presents enough of a hitch in the usual way of doing business that it is often an opportunity for reflection and planning.

- When there is a specific problem. A specific problem is different from a general crisis. The problem may be clearer and its resolution more effective if addressed in the broader context of an overall planning process.

- If your organizational environment is disrupted. A disruption may be a new competitor, a change in funding guidelines, a political or economic change in your community, or something else. In any case, it requires taking stock and responding, and may be a good occasion for planning.

- Before launching a new venture. The opportunity for planning may occur as you decide whether or not to launch a new venture or during the launch itself. In either case, there will be an impact on the organization that may cause you to think more broadly about organizational plans and purposes.

- As an ongoing process. This is not a periodic work stoppage for planning. It is more an attitude of forethought, a disposition to reflect on the possibilities and consequences of various directions and actions.

The planning process: two models to consider

Getting where you want to go and allowing for side trips is not just a family vacation dilemma. Organizational life is a constant balancing act between the destination-bound and side trippers, between the importance of staying focused and on track and the equal importance of experimenting and opening up new territory. Good planning equips an organization for both, and good leadership partners insist on the co-existence of directness and diversion.

The planning process itself needs to be well-focused and tightly organized with equal amounts of creativity and humor. As you devise your own planning process from the two models that follow, don't forget the focused part or the fun part.

Most organizations can use the rejuvenating effects of a spring tonic from time to time. Good planning ought to result not merely in efficient implementation but in implementation characterized by vigor and even passion. The two models that follow in summary fashion are: planning as an agenda for action and planning as an organizational tonic.

1. Planning as an agenda for action.

Focus: Specific organizational and programmatic accomplishment.

Planning period: One to three years

Participants: 15–25 people (or a number you feel okay about working together in one group)

Time required: Four to six hours of full group, four to six hours in preparation by a leadership group of three to five.

Advantages: Is relatively quick, focuses on tangible items, forges a consensus, pays attention to what we want to do versus what we should do or historically have done, or what might be interesting.

Disadvantages: Requires quick decision-making that may be uncomfortable for those who work best with more reflection; also may cause concern among those uncomfortable with a "let's just try it for a year or so" attitude.

This is an agenda for action planning—quick, non-detailed, focused on the present energy of the board, and oriented around doing. It may be worth thinking about and worth trying in some form for a year.

2. Planning as an organizational tonic

This approach is not precisely aimed at what your organization should do or when or how it should be done. Rather, it is directed at assisting the organizational leadership to connect and reconnect with the initial dream, enthusiasm, or fire that gave birth to your agency. Such a return to the beginnings will focus and revitalize the efforts of your organization. Any good planning activity should do the same.

Focus: The essential enthusiasm that initiated the organization, the continuing enthusiasms that drive the present leadership

Planning period: One year

Participants: The board

Time required: Two hours of reflective time

Advantages: The strength is in re-focusing, re-energizing and re-committing board leadership

Disadvantages: This method will not deliver specifics but will provide a livelier context in which decisions about specific objectives will be easier and better made

Setting and mood are crucial for this conversation. It might get done well in one and a half hours. It won't get done at all if your board is feeling plagued by pressing decisions or the execution of business details. Board members who tend to be fairly task-oriented may need a rationale for "this much time spent just philosophizing." A reasonable rationale goes something like, "We always seem to have too much to do and often find ourselves spending efforts on activities not central to what we are about. Today we are going to work to clarify that essential purpose so we make better decisions about time and resources." Or, "We seem to use a lot of energy on the structures and procedures we have devised to carry out what it is we really are about. Let's make sure we remember what this is and give that special enthusiasm more attention."

Reviewing and evaluating

Crucial to the planning process are the steps of reviewing and evaluating. We have talked about the board evaluating itself in Chapter 3 and we will talk about evaluating the executive in Chapter 18. A third important kind of evaluation to be done is related to programs and services as described in your organizational plan.

Here are four tips from our own experience:

1. Planning documents are sometimes so long that actual dates, amounts, and numbers get lost. Pull those out and have them available for review.

2. Put someone in charge of keeping the board focused on the plans they made and how the organization is doing relative to those plans.

3. A once-a-year look at implementation as it relates to the plan is probably not enough, but every board meeting would get tiresome. Try checking in two to four times a year on how the organization is performing relative to the plans made. At that time, you might also choose to update the plan by making needed adjustments.

4. Consider a three-year planning cycle. A one-year plan is not long enough, but a five-year plan is probably too long for how fast things change.

In summary, with luck and large doses of persistence and imagination, the board will be able to have a satisfying planning process. However, everyone needs to be reminded that planning and evaluation are most powerfully construed as an attitude rather than specific events. Of course, occasionally you will want to take a pause in your hectic organizational life for an intentional planning process, because your agency likely will be more vital and more on target if the planning and evaluation attitude regularly permeates your activity. Instead of storing them away for three years, the best evaluation questions and the most thoughtful planning processes ought to be encouraged in the middle of a board meeting, executive evaluation, or discussion about new officers.

We urge you to develop your own best planning and evaluation putting reflection in the middle of action and dropping big questions in the middle of small tactics. Use whatever bits and pieces from this section that work best for you. Fashion a plan that you can feel positive about infusing into the life of your organization, but don't forget the good questions you asked and the thoughtful discussions you had along the way. Those conversations are worth remembering and repeating. That's the planning and evaluation attitude indicative of healthy organizations.

Chapter 8

Staffing Matters

At a time when most people think that bigger is better, it is hard not to believe that having staff is a sign that you are "grown up" as an organization. That may or may not be the case. We know some people who have been in their organization for a long time and remember the early days without staff, when board members were all engaged and enthused. Those, they say, were the best times. Regardless of whether an organization has paid staff, its primary goal should be maintaining faithfulness to the mission and doing the good work that it was established to do. That may mean a change from a $20,000 a year budget and no paid staff to a $200,000 a year budget and three staff. Too often we have seen small organizations strain too much to get bigger and not enough to get better. We like the idea of working first for better. If that leads to bigger, fine. If it does not, then make sure you take full satisfaction in what good things you already do.

Growth may not be your challenge. You may need to think through how better to divide the work among the two full-time and two part-time people you currently have as staff. First of all, if you have an executive, make sure she is in the lead on this. As a board member you can consult, even advise if asked, but your own primary responsibility for staff is with the executive. It is the executive who manages the rest of the staff.

In what follows there are some guidelines and suggestions on how to think about staffing. You can and should help, support, and now and again advise the executive about this very important part of the life of your organization. What we have to say is organized into two brief sections: people and hours, and pay and benefits.

PEOPLE AND HOURS

You may be surprised to know that at your local school and community college, salaries and benefits make up 80–85% of the budget. That is usual for education across our nation, and if you think about the job of education, it makes sense. However, it probably isn't right for your not-for-profit organization. Generally, what you spend on staff should be in the range of 50–60% of your total budget. For example, if you have an annual budget of $50,000 you'll be fine spending $25,000–$30,000 on staff. If you are at $200,000 then $100,000 to $120,000.

Let's stick with the numbers for a while. Say you determine you can spend $60,000 on staff. You might assume that means a director at $25,000, a program and marketing person at $20,000 and an administrative support person at $15,000. In that model you would have three full-time people, and for many organizations, hiring only full-time employees seems right. We propose, however, that that philosophy is similar to the "volunteers can't be trusted" philosophy. In other words, you may want to consider utilizing some part-time people.

In any case, we urge you to be creative and flexible about the staffing issue. We know of very successful half-time executives and very effective staffs where people work 16, 20, and 32 hours a week. Let's consider the previous example. A totally different way to divide up a $60,000 staffing budget would be as follows. The executive works four-day weeks, or 80% time, costing $20,000. One person focuses on programs 60% of the time. Another person spends 60% time on marketing and public relations, leaving $16,000 to hire a full-time administrative person who can help with all the administrative duties.

That may seem complicated but here's what it gets you: more people with more focus on specific tasks. It also gets you people whose varied and complicated lives are respected—employees who don't have to choose between work and home, work and hobbies, or work and consulting. Our experience is you can often get better people when you offer flexibility. We think it is worth thinking about, trying, and then of course evaluating to see how it is going.

PAY AND BENEFITS

The issue of pay was partially addressed in the previous section. Here's an additional word about salary levels. While there are national studies about how much executives are paid in not-for-profit organizations, these studies may not be applicable to your community. In short, you need to be reasonable relative to your total budget and fair to those doing the work. One way to get at that is check with your local funders to see if they have collected comparative salary data. You may have to go to your state arts council or state not-for-profit association. Usually salaries vary most by size of budget, so if you are an $80,000 agency you need not pay at the same salary level as one with a $300,000 budget. Rather than merely paying what is fair, you may choose to be a leader in salary scales for an organization your size. That choice might cost only $2,000 a year, but it sends an extremely positive message about the importance of our work.

It is possible that you may not be in a position to have monetary benefits other than those that are required. The required ones are unemployment insurance, workers compensation, and 50% of social security. The three of those need to be equal to 10% to 12.5% of whatever salary you are paying. Increasingly, agencies are setting aside an additional 10 to 15% for other benefits. Those would include health care and retirement (for which an employee does not pay tax) and child-care and education (on which they will probably need to pay tax).

Choices are good. If you have a program that pays 10% on top of mandatory benefits for health care and the employee does not need health care because he is covered under the plan of his spouse, the organization may save money but the employee loses for lack of a choice. One agency we know with a budget of $240,000 offers choices to everyone so that all get the benefit of the benefits. The chart that follows shows how that can be computed. You may want to adapt it for your situation.

One last issue related to pay and benefits is that of contracts. Generally they are for one year and, unless you are a large agency, in the form of a letter of agreement. This letter specifies the tasks, the hours, and the salary and benefits. It is of course signed by both the employee and the executive director. Again, a sample that you may wish to adapt follows.

Staff Benefit Computation

Employee_____ Date _____

Mandatory	I*	II*	III*
Social security/Medicare	7.65	7.65	7.65
Workers Compensation	2.6	2.6	2.6
Unemployment Insurance	2.0	2.0	2.0
Mandatory benefits	**12.25**	**12.25**	**12.25**

Optional (non-taxed)
Medical	____	____	____
Retirement	____	____	____
Disability	____	____	____
Total optional	**____**	**____**	**____**

Optional/Taxed
Education	____	____	____
Child Care	____	____	____
Total optional/taxed	**____**	**____**	**____**

Grand total benefit package	**24%**	**25%**	**26%**

Dollar value of total benefit package	____	____	____
Less total mandatory and optional benefits	____	____	____
Balance remaining of benefits package	**____**	**____**	**____**

Vacation and Personal Leave

Vacation	Two weeks; after three years, three weeks (must expend each year)
Personal/sick leave	Two weeks (may accumulate up to 12 days as carry-over)

*Categories:	I	Administrative Assistants
	II	Directors, Program areas and Financial Officer
	III	Executive Director

December 1, 2002

To: Ralph Smith

What follows is an outline of my understanding about your professional employment with The Morrison Center. If it seems to you to be a satisfactory description, please sign and return one copy, keeping one for your own records.

Title: Coordinator of Marketing and Development

Responsibilities: Coordinate all aspects of marketing and fundraising and from time to time assist the executive director with special projects.

Reporting: You will report directly to the executive director.

Salary and benefits: The annualized salary is $32,000. Your position is half time and therefore $16,000. The benefits include 2 weeks vacation and 1 week sick leave each year. 10% of gross salary will be made available to you for health insurance, retirement, or education. These benefits will begin three months after your start date of January 1.

Time period: This arrangement is for the period January 1, 2003 through December 31, 2003. You will have a performance and salary review in October of 2003 for changes and adjustment for the time period beginning January 1, 2004.

I am very pleased to have you join us here at The Morrison Center at this important time in the life of our agency.

Sincerely,   With approval,

Barbara Jones, Executive Director   Ralph Smith
Date: Date:

Chapter 9

The IRS and Budgets

This chapter is not only about April 15, and it is probably not one of those chapters you can skip. If we have managed to get your attention, here's the first thing we want to say. Other than watching over an organization's faithfulness to its mission, watching over the budget is easily the next most important task you have. You don't have to be a math wizard or a certified public accountant to do what is required of you as a board member. There are many reasons why financial management is important, not the least of which is the Internal Revenue Service. In this chapter as well as in chapters 12 and 13, we discuss rules and regulations that come from the IRS and the State Offices of the Attorney General. These matters change, and they often vary from state to state. You may want to check with your local attorney or accountant.

Your organization has been given a very big advantage. If you are not-for-profit, the IRS has given you a "Letter of Determination" which grants you status as a 501(c)(3) organization with special privileges. If you are an association, religious institution, or foundation, other rules may apply. Not-for-profit organizations have the following advantages:

1. Exemption from federal corporate income tax on earnings related to your organization's purpose.
2. In most states exemption from property and sales tax on purchases.
3. Exemption from federal unemployment tax.
4. Deductibility of donations from individuals.
5. Eligibility for grants from foundation and government agencies.

Besides those very important privileges, the board is assigned the responsibility of accounting for funds and seeing that all are being utilized for the tax exempt purposes of the organization. Apart from such obvious matters as misspending funds (fraud) and failure to keep records of income and expenses, there are two other issues to which you should pay particular attention: unrelated business income and lobbying.

UNRELATED BUSINESS INCOME

As long as you are receiving funds from programs, events, and services that directly relate to your tax-exempt purpose you are fine. Income you receive from activities that are substantially unrelated to your purpose is either not permitted or is taxable. That situation would put you into unfair competition with for-profit businesses that of course must pay tax. For example, if you are a senior center you probably can't open a retail bookstore that has no direct relationship to serving seniors.

LOBBYING

You can as board members or staff of a not-for-profit organization advocate with lawmakers at all levels of government for legislation, policies, and regulations that are beneficial to the people you serve or to your own organization or sector. The federal government has supported lobbying by not-for-profit organizations since 1976 with legislation by Congress revising the laws governing lobbying. In 1990 the IRS issued regulations that carried out the spirit and the letter of that earlier legislation. What you cannot do though is contribute money to, or publicly promote, a candidate who is running for office.

Many good social changes have come about in part by not-for-profit organizations advocating for a cause. Mothers Against Drunk Driving, health organizations lobbying for anti-smoking legislation, and environmental groups advocating clean air and water all are examples of not-for-profit organizations that have used their right to lobby to make changes that benefit the community at large. If you have any further questions you should consult your state Ethics Commission.

BUILDING A BUDGET

Ordinarily the executive would take the lead on this together with the treasurer of the board or the board finance committee. Some large organizations have a paid financial officer who likely would have a lead role as well. We think that since the board has final responsibility to monitor how funds are spent, it is best if they too are closely involved in putting the budget together in the first place. This will help them to better understand it since they are more likely to take serious responsibility for what they have helped create.

The easy way to build a budget is to take last year's budget and increase everything by three to five percent. If times are tough, you may need to decrease everything by three to five percent or more. That method has the advantage of being simple, but it has the disadvantage of assuming that every line-item (salaries, program expense, and utilities) continues to be of equal importance. An alternative method is to start with those fixed items such as rent, utilities, loan payments, etc., add them up, and then see what is left and determine how you wish to spend it. This method has the advantage of combining reality (what must be paid) with flexibility for the remaining line items.

Another way to build a budget is to start with programs: what do we want to do next year and what will it cost? The assumption with this method is that everything is up for discussion and that the core programs and services can be recreated. This approach may naturally grow out of a planning process. It has the advantage of making sure the money goes to what you currently believe is most important. If you decide to budget based on programs, we suggest it is better to do so as part of a three-year plan rather than annually. You need to decide which way or combination of ways you wish to adopt and then make sure that as many board members as possible are included in the building and approving of the budget.

REPORTS

If not monthly, at least quarterly you as a board member should receive, review, and fully understand how the income is coming in and the money is being spent. This is not merely the job of the treasurer or the finance committee. They may be in the lead in assembling and presenting the reports but you must understand the full financial situation. This is the one thing that may or may not be satisfying to you as a board member, but it is crucial.

Let's take a look at a typical line item budget.

Income

1. First list income from your programs and services. That might include admissions, fees, sales, contracts, etc. We suggest that these items (sometimes called earned income) equal about 50% of your budget.

2. Second, list income from grants, including government, foundations, third party agencies like the United Way, and arts councils. The more of this that goes to general operating support versus new project support the better. Getting money by having to create new projects that result in more work is a mixed blessing. If you get new money and spend it all on new expenses, you're losing ground.

3. Next, list funds from individuals and corporations. Individuals may make regular donations to an annual fund. Corporate funds are most often applied to specified events or programs.

4. Finally, list any fund-raising events that you intend. Here put the gross or total amount you expect to raise, then make sure in the expenses column that the costs of this event are listed. Also make sure that the income versus expenses figure makes the event worth doing.

Expenses

Begin by listing personnel expenses, first including full- and part-time staff, then consultants and outside contractors. Other usual items to include are:

- Program and service expenses
- Marketing and public relations
- Occupancy expenses: utilities, rent or mortgage, cleaning
- Office equipment and supplies
- Communications, fax, telephone, mail, internet expenses
- Travel – staff and outside consultants, etc.
- Insurance – property and liability
- Printing and duplication
- Design and publication

All of the above may not apply to your organization and in some cases additional expenses are incurred that relate to the special services and programs you offer.

There are many ways to do a regular monthly or quarterly report. Here are two simple ways that we think get the job done and are easily understandable by even non-financial people.

A to Z Center
Financial Report 2002

For month ending June 30

Budget Items	Annual Budget	Budgeted Year to Date	Actual Income & Expense to Date	Variance	Notes
Income*					
Fees and contracts	40,000	20,000	16,500	(3,500)	Big season is Sept. – Nov.
Community found.	15,000	5,000	10,000	5,000	100% of funds
Individuals	12,000	6,000	0	(6,000)	Annual fund comes in Nov.
Etc.					
Expenses*					
Personnel					
Executive director	25,000	12,500	12,500	0	
Program director	20,000	10,000	10,000	0	
Administrative asst.	15,000	7,500	7,500	0	
Etc.					

*These are general categories for the purpose of illustration. You will have your own categories.

Neighborhood Health Center
Financial Report 2002*

For the twelve months ending December 31

	Current Month Actual	Current Month Budget	Year to Date Actual	Year to Date Budget	Annual Budget
Income					
Contributions	26,000	4,000	46,600	48,000	48,000
Special events	0	2,000	27,000	24,000	24,000
Sponsorships	0	2,500	32,000	30,000	30,000
Etc.					
Expenses					
Salaries	8,075	8,333	96,400	100,000	100,000
Benefits	1,542	1,666	18,800	20,000	20,000
Rent	1,000	1,000	12,000	12,000	12,000
Etc.					

*In this format you would use one page to list your expenses and a separate page for your income.

These two reports seem to indicate there are no real budgetary problems within the organizations. If, for example, contributions or contract income were falling short in a certain month, you should ask whether that is the result of a specific problem or simply a seasonal difference. On the expense side, if salaries are running over, you need to ask whether it is a problem or the result of additional salary costs for a new program.

Note that the example of the Neighborhood Health Center provides quite a bit more detail and the board may decide it wants to have more information by which to monitor how the finances are going.

AUDITS

Audits are necessary but maybe not every year if you have a budget under $100,000. They need to be done by a certified public accountant who is fully independent and not on your board or related to someone on it. If you are on a calendar year budget you will usually have all the financial records from the bank by the end of January. The audit will likely take four to six weeks and should be available by the end of March or three months after the end of your fiscal year. Make sure you have copies available for all major funders.

Chapter 10

Sources of Funds

P resumably you are a board member because you believe your organization can make your community a better place. Believing that, you will undoubtedly be talking with others about supporting your organization. Those conversations will lead you to meet fine and generous people who, like you, want to feel a part of an organization working to make life better in your part of the world. That's the inspiring part.

The more challenging part is finding ways to raise all the money you need to do what is so important. First, of course, you won't have to approach this task starting from scratch. There are revenue sources already in place. Whether your budget is $40,000 or $400,000, some of that money comes into your organization on a fairly dependable basis. But there is always additional money to be raised. Here are some ways for you to think about and act on the task of creating revenue for your organization.

THREE WAYS TO CREATE REVENUE

In looking at the big picture of creating revenue, here's a way to think about it that may help you get your arms around this crucial and complex task.

Try thinking of all the ways that funds come into your organization in three broad categories: products and services, grants and donations, and fundraisers and special events. After explaining what each includes, we'll suggest some percent of the total income you may want to assign to each, and finally offer our own sense about the advantages and disadvantages of the methods of raising funds presented in each of the three categories.

Products and services are anything you do as part of your mission from which income is derived. They may be tangible items or they may be programs. Most often this category results from fees, admissions, sales, or dues. Grants and donations generate revenue in support of the work you do rather than for the products or services you produce. This category would include money received from individuals, foundations, corporations, and government agencies. Fundraisers and special events bring in funds as a result of efforts other than the work of your mission, such as raffles, auctions, golf outings, and tennis matches.

This overall picture of revenue sources is one way to grasp all the activity that goes into the creation of revenue for your organization. Now let's look a little deeper at each of the three categories.

Products and services

The products of your organization, whether classes, counseling, or concerts, are a legitimate part of your revenue-creation work. While they are not usually thought of as fundraising, they do in fact raise funds for your organization, and we find it useful to think of them as part of the total effort toward providing necessary income. We have heard some board members say that they have a goal of creating 50% of their annual income from the work of the organization. That may be low. We know of one science museum that for years received 90% of its budget from admissions. We know of a historic preservation district that receives over 90% of its total income from lease arrangements. When the work that flows from your mission creates a large portion of your revenue, fundraising is easier; there is a desirable economy of effort within your organization. If, on the other hand, you have to do the work of your mission and rely on doing a majority of the work of fund development by other means, that requires more of everyone. It could require more employees or more volunteers.

For some, however, the 50% goal for products and services may be too high. If you are doing job readiness and placement services with out-of-school youth, you may be in a situation where the clients can't pay the full cost and the government has cut the funding. Serving those who do not have the personal resources to pay does not, however, translate into no income from services. Oftentimes a third party, usually local or state government, will provide funds on a fee-for-contract basis. In any case, funds which come to your organization because of the work you do enable you to focus both your programmatic and fund-creation efforts in the same activity. That is a good place to be.

Grants and donations

As you strive to generate revenue in support of what you do, remember that most donations will come from individuals. Generally these individuals come to support your organization in one of three ways: they give through an annual fund, they give to support or sponsor a specific activity or program, or they participate in planned giving. All these require staff and often board members' time and attention to build relationships and, in the case of planned giving, may require special information or assistance.

An annual fund we know about raises 10% of the organization's budget of $600,000. What they do is send out about 4,000 letters in October with a form on which are giving levels of $40 to over $5,000. The letter is personal and tells the story of the work they do. It is short, colorful, and reminds those who receive it that this is a once-a-year request. About 300 families respond and then a follow-up postcard is sent early in December to a select group of 1,500. Another 100 or so respond to this request. The cost is about $1,800 for the two mailings' printing, postage, and mailing service. The executive director spends about four to five hours writing the two requests. Support staff donate another four hours to organizing the lists and printed materials and getting them to the printer and mailing service. You don't need a very sharp pencil to compute that spending $1,800 cash and about eight hours of staff time to raise $60,000 is a good return.

There are three or four points to underline from this story. First, it requires that your organization create and maintain a mailing list of people who care about your work. Second, if you do say it is a once-a-year request, guarantee that is the case and make it happen once a year at the same time so it will be expected. Third, it is yet more effective if board members write personal notes or make personal phone calls or visits to selected individuals. Finally, not in the story as first told is the fact that this organization has a small core of volunteers who send out thank you notes on postcards, handwritten and signed. This may seem a little hard to do and organize, but it is a big boost to repeat giving, and if done promptly, a memorable touch unfortunately done by too few.

In terms of a combination of cash and return on investment, it doesn't get much better than that annual letter illustration. But there are in almost every community individuals capable of giving in excess of

$10,000 who genuinely care about the work you do. Usually this requires no cash expenditure but rather requires considerable time to identify and cultivate these friends. *People give to people.* Potential donors must get to know and trust you—some say there should be six contacts before an ask. Again, this requires staff planning and execution. The larger the organization the more detailed, time consuming, and expensive the task. Board members have a role here: seeing that this level of fundraising is done to begin with and then helping to cultivate the best prospects. Just as important is seeing that those all-important thank you notes are sent promptly.

Planned giving is another form of donation. There are entire books on this subject alone. In short, you should explore it, even though it will not produce revenue until well into the future and must be handled on a very personal basis. For example, one organization started with its board and rather quickly got 25% of its members (in that case, four) to name the organization in their will or in a fund at the local community foundation. Then those few members talked about what they had done to a few more long-time supporters. Though it is a slow and mostly quiet process, it is likely to be worth the effort it will take. And again, the larger the organization, the larger the effort.

As a board member you will not only have some direct involvement in individual giving but will also need to be involved in pursuing corporations for donations and sponsorships. There is not much magic here. Most corporations will sponsor events or programs where they receive substantial name recognition. They of course are more apt to be interested where their own customers or employees are involved or where their services or products relate in some positive way to your services and products. We probably need not remind you that they may also be willing to give away their services (attorneys, accountants) or the products they produce or sell (computers, desks). Here the expenditure is again more related to time than money. And that time is related to the slow, careful process of building relationships and writing good letters, reports, and thank you's.

Speaking of writing, grant writing can also provide revenue to an organization. As a board member you should be sure your organization has explored the possibilities. Most grants will be secured through foundations and government agencies, and oftentimes the writing process involves extensive forms and attachments that require anywhere from

20 to 80 hours of work. Two small hints: Don't overestimate the technique of proposal writing and don't underestimate the importance of pre-proposal talking and corresponding. Good grant writing is mostly clear and complete thinking and writing. If your staff is sending out blind proposals, like sending out blind resumes for jobs, it probably won't work. As a rule, the likelihood of funding—as well as the amount—can be determined up front if you spend thoughtful time with the foundation program officers. You need to know and be known by them. Spending extensive time where there is at least a 50-50 chance of a positive response is what you want your organization to be doing.

Fundraisers and special events

We put this category last because in order of what you should be doing and assisting others to do, that is where it belongs. If most of your time can be spent focusing on obtaining funds from the admissions, fees, and sales that result from the programs and projects of your organization, you will save time and money. If another significant amount of income can come from those individuals, foundations, government agencies, and corporations who have one reason or another to care about what you are doing, that is good as well. If you must create other ways to convince people to spend their money in a way that benefits the work of your organization, do it thoughtfully. It may prove to be necessary but it isn't greatly desirable. There is nothing inherently wrong with special events, auctions, and golf outings, but they do run three risks:

1. You may become better known for the event than for your organization and its mission.

2. You may exhaust staff and/or volunteers on this non-mission related activity.

3. You may end up with a sizable income but likewise sizable expense and, therefore, very little net positive result.

If you can design a special event that sounds like your mission, does not take hundreds of hours of staff and volunteer time, and brings you substantial net income, then it just may be worth doing.

In summary, we offer the following percentages of income based on our own experience, realizing that your situation may call for a different plan.

Products and services: 40–60% of income

Grants and donations: 30–40% of income

Fundraisers and special events: 10–20% of income

In any case, these suggested percentages can form the basis for a thoughtful conversation among the board, executive, and those in your organization responsible for bringing in the income. Then you can decide together what works for your organization and exactly what kind of a fund development system you wish to have for your organization.

Chapter 11

Rainy Day Funds
and Endowments

Y ou probably know that, with family budgets, it is important to have three or four months' worth of salary in some kind of account where it can be easily accessed. The same goes for organizations. If you have an annual budget of $120,000, you should try to establish an account with $30,000 to $40,000. It is more important with this kind of account that the funds are accessible, not necessarily that they are earning a lot of interest. This money needs to be easily available when a fund-raising event gets cancelled, a furnace gives out, or a funder decides they aren't funding your kind of programs anymore. If you don't like the sound of rainy day fund, you can call it something fancy like working capital reserve. It is working a little (making a small amount of interest), and it is in reserve (meaning you don't raid it on a monthly basis).

Our experience is that most organizations get started on such a fund in one of three ways. They might have a particularly good year and end up with a balance of $11,000 on their $120,000 budget, and decide to put $6,000 aside for that rainy day and keep the $5,000 for balance to take care of cash flow during the next year. A second possibility is that a fundraising event scheduled to make $4,000 ends up clearing $7,000 because all the food gets donated. Thirdly, there is the situation where a beloved retired schoolteacher dies and leaves your organization $40,000. After lots of discussion, it is decided that $30,000 will go to the working capital reserve fund and the $10,000 balance would be used to start an endowment fund.

Your own rainy day fund may get started in any number of ways. The important thing is to get it started.

ENDOWMENTS

An endowment fund is simply money invested in a way that makes enough money so that the fund grows and so that some of the proceeds can be applied to the yearly income of the organization. There is, of course, much more to be said, and we will try saying it by answering four questions:

1. Are there different kinds of endowments?
2. How is an endowment set up and who manages the money?
3. How much money from the endowment can be spent?
4. How will it grow?

1. Are there different kinds of endowments?

There are basically two kinds of endowments: unrestricted and designated. Unrestricted means that the earnings from the fund may be used for whatever purpose the board decides. One year it could be used for a new outreach program, another year it could be used for a new telephone system. This kind of fund offers maximum flexibility, including the option of using it as a general income item for operating expense.

Designated funds are those in which the earnings are used only for a specified purpose. Some funds are designated for new programs, some for landscaping and trees, some for projects related to families below the poverty level. The way this kind of fund usually gets started is that a donor has given or left in a will funds to be applied toward something about which they themselves care deeply. Often it is the case that an endowment will have two or more funds: some designated or restricted to certain purposes and some unrestricted and therefore available for whatever the board decides. While all endowment funds can be kept in the same investments, they must of course be accounted for separately.

2. How do we set up an endowment and who manages the money?

Once you as a board decide that the time is right and you have a rainy day fund safely established, you can begin the process of setting up an endowment. You will want to decide upon and record a few key policies. They should include what the unrestricted funds may be used for, who will manage the money, what kinds of investments you wish to include in your portfolio, which board members will oversee the investment managers (often a treasurer and at least three people who have some personal or professional experience with investments), and what percent of the total amount you will utilize and on what schedule.

The policies may also include some guidelines and suggestions for increasing the endowment and perhaps a target goal for five or ten years.

The way in which the endowment funds are managed is an important decision. Some organizations are large enough to set up a separate foundation board. Generally, whoever manages the funds, you will want to diversify where they are invested. Most organizations would want a mix of stocks, mutual funds, bonds, and money market funds. Usually, it is best for organizations to be a bit more conservative than a thirty-six year-old individual with thirty more years of income ahead. As with most decisions, there are advantages and disadvantages to consider when deciding how the fund will be managed. Sometimes, newly created endowment funds (lets say $25,000 to $100,000) are managed by a committee of board members who are particularly knowledgeable. In this case no fees are paid to those managing the endowment, but the relationship with the rest of the board may become strained if the investments don't perform well. Another option is to have someone outside the board manage your endowment—a bank investment company or a community foundation.

Banks and investment firms have professionals who specialize in creating and managing endowment accounts. There is of course a fee for this service. Still, a small committee of the board needs to be actively involved in overseeing the performance of the managers from the bank or investment firm.

Sometimes boards will have their endowment fund managed by a community foundation. Here as well there will be a fee and here as well you should be able to receive high-quality professional service. One other advantage is that a community foundation feels like a more established and safe place to secure your investment.

You should carefully review all the options in your community before deciding. Endowments can be a very important source of ongoing support for your organization. That's a good reason for you to spend some time thinking it all through.

3. How much money from the endowment can be spent?

The fact is that unless the fund is designated and restricted to a certain percentage, you can spend whatever you wish. Some decide on spending a certain percent of the proceeds. For example, if you decide to spend 50% of the proceeds, and the proceeds earned are 4%, you spend 2%. In a particularly good year with 16% proceeds, you spend 8%.

Many boards set an amount that relates to the total endowment, which could be a large or small percentage. However, if you spent 10%, or even 7%, unless you are adding large amounts your fund will dwindle and eventually disappear. One rule of thumb that has worked well for many endowments over the years is to set a policy that the board may decide on a percent every budget year that is up to 5% of the average balance in the endowment over the last three years. It is the "up to" phrase that is crucial, because it puts a cap on the total amount and insures that the funds will continue to grow. That same phrase also permits the board in particularly good years in the budget to utilize only 3% or less and enable the endowment fund to grow more rapidly.

If you decide on the 5% number as previously mentioned and your average endowment balance over the past three years is $60,000, you may spend $3,000 a year. It also means that as you calculate how much it takes to create or add to an endowment, you see that whatever income you hope for you must multiply by 20 to get the amount of endowment investment required. For example, if I wish to have $1,000 a month or $12,000 annually, I will need to have twenty times that, or $240,000, in the endowment.

4. How will it grow?

First, the endowment is likely to grow automatically if you spend 5% or less each year. In addition, you may decide that some percentage of any excess funds at the end of a budget year will also be placed in the endowment. The endowment will grow faster yet if you decide for the first three years to take none of the proceeds. Endowments grow most of all from special donations from people who care about the future of the organization. Some organizations decide to have an endowment campaign. If they do, they make sure it does not interfere with the donations necessary to fund the annual budget. They also give the option for people to make donations directly into the fund, often on a two- or three-year basis, or to make donations resulting from designation in a will or an insurance policy. The latter is called planned giving, meaning there is a plan to give in the future versus an actual gift in the present.

You may or may not be ready for an endowment fund. You are probably not ready until you have a solid rainy day fund set. But creating an endowment fund is not only good future financial planning, it says to your community, "We plan on being here a long time."

Chapter 12

Incorporation and By-laws

There is a lot of legal detail about not-for-profit organizations that you don't need to know. However, there are two specific things you should understand: incorporation and by-laws. You need to understand them because they already exist in your organization and probably could benefit from being reviewed. On the other hand, if you are starting a new organization, you will need to create them. What we have to say here is not a substitute for good legal advice. You probably will need a lawyer to deal with the papers of incorporation, though you may get by without one to do the writing of your by-laws. What follows is basic and in outline form. If you wish to know a whole lot more, check out one of the books listed in the Suggested Readings section at the back of the book or consult your friendly attorney.

What you are doing with incorporation papers and by-laws is setting the basic ground rules by which your organization will do its work. While by-laws can be changed (though usually not without a two-thirds vote of the board), articles of incorporation are less easily changeable because they involve the state government.

ON INCORPORATION

The Articles of Incorporation are the basic document, or birth certificate of a not-for-profit organization. These are sometimes also called the Corporate Charter. The life of a not-for-profit organization really begins when these incorporating articles are filed with the state government, usually in the Attorney General's office. Once this is done, they are binding unless changed by a somewhat difficult and time-consuming process. Our advice is to get it right the first time. Once done you may not by law engage in any activities that are not specifically stated in the incorporation papers. It is also important that you write the articles in such a way as to permit the broadest flexibility of activities connected to your mission.

If the organization is not a religious congregation, there are two different ways to incorporate: either as a public service organization or a membership organization. The majority of not-for-profit organizations fall in the first category. Public service organizations exist to serve some broad public good or group like senior adults, bluegrass music, or mental health. When the primary purpose of the organization is to serve the public, there will generally be a board of trustees that is self-perpetuating, that nominates and elects its own members.

Membership organizations are in business to serve their members rather than the general public. Most common in this category are professional and trade associations who serve their members with information, publications, professional development, meetings, and conferences. In this case, the board is elected by the membership and responsible to them to carry out the mission of the organization.

While it is true that public service organizations often have membership support groups who raise funds or do events, the organization still remains directed toward the public in general and not members. Likewise, membership associations will often take on projects that benefit the public, like food and clothing drives. However, the organization's basic mission remains directed at the members and not at the general public.

ON BY-LAWS

Most of the time you'll inherit by-laws, not have to create them. Unfortunately, too much of the time it will be difficult to locate a copy. That will give you some clue about their importance in the organization. Early in your term on the board, you should know what they say. You should also understand what it takes to revise or suspend them, generally, two-thirds vote of the board. If the by-laws seem too restrictive or no longer appropriate, identify some board members who appreciate both detail and simplicity and produce a revision for board approval.

Pay particular attention to those sections of the by-laws that deal with board membership. How are potential board members identified? How are they elected? For what term of office? May they be reelected and on what grounds may they be removed? Generally, by-laws with flexibility are most workable when they contain phrases such as, "up to 24 board members," "up to ten meetings a year," and "there shall be an executive committee and whatever program and administrative committees that from time to time seem important and necessary."

Get sample by-laws from other organizations about your size that you respect. Don't make a by-law revision process the centerpiece of several board meetings. In our experience, by-laws are most important when they enable you to do the administrative and programmatic work you need to do with a maximum of efficiency and ease.

By-laws go beyond the Articles of Incorporation in that they explain how the organization is to be governed. They are for the board and usually do not have to be filed with the state or be approved by anyone outside the organization. In reviewing or writing by-laws it is important to make sure they are complete. That is, they need to cover all the basic issues that affect how your board and organization conducts its business. A good reference is *The Nonprofit Board's Guide to By-laws* by Kim Arthur Zeitlin and Susan F. Dorn published by BoardSource (which, by the way, is an excellent resource). They have produced far more good detail than we can include here. We do, however, include for your consideration their list of items that should be addressed in your by-law statements.

1. General
- Official name of the organization
- Location of principal office
- Statement of purposes
- Any limitations required for tax exemption, such as prohibitions against political campaign participation and inurement or private foundation provisions for 501(c)(3) organizations.
- Procedure for amending the by-laws
- Procedure for dissolving the organization
- Disposition of assets upon dissolution

2. Board of Directors

- Number of members
- Qualifications for membership
- Terms of office and term limits
- Selection process
- Process for filling vacancies
- Frequency of meetings
- Quorum requirements
- Powers of the executive committee
- Descriptions and powers of other standing committees
- Meeting procedures (such as action without a meeting and meeting by telephone)
- Compensation
- Circumstances under which directors may be removed

3. Officers

- Qualifications for holding office
- Duties of officers
- Process for selecting or appointing officers
- Term and term limits
- Provision for a chief executive (if not an officer)
- Circumstances under which officers may be removed

4. Members (this section may not apply to your organization)

- Qualifications for membership
- Admission procedures
- Dues obligations of members
- Classes of membership and their rights and privileges
- Notice required for membership meetings
- Quorum requirements
- Frequency of meetings and meeting procedures
- Circumstances under which members may be expelled
- Voting procedures

5. Fiscal matters

- Audit committee and audits
- Duties of treasurer
- Indemnification

In summary, the Articles of Incorporation and by-laws taken together form the basis for the conduct of your organization. For that reason they are very significant and need to be carefully written and faithfully followed. In most organizations, once they are completed it is not necessary to review them for any amendment more often than every three years. On a yearly basis they remain an important touchstone for the life of your organization.

Chapter 13

Rules, Reports and Records

T his may not be the chapter you'll remember as "high on inspiration." Rather, the objective is to gather into one place all the items needed to stay legal and on the good side of the state attorney general's office and Internal Revenue Service. Actually, there aren't very many and, for organizations with no staff and/or a budget under $10,000, there are even fewer. For those organizations, there are some other items included here which, though not legally required, do make for a neat and tidy organization.

Here's the outline of the chapter. First is a note about what it really means to be not-for-profit. Following that is a section on the rules and reports that, depending on the organization's size, are important to have in mind as the year progresses. For that section, a sample calendar of deadlines and dates not to be missed is included. Thirdly is a section on liability and finally, a section on records and the what, who, and how of keeping them.

WHAT IT MEANS TO BE NOT-FOR-PROFIT

There are three sectors in American society: the government sector, the for-profit sector, and the not-for-profit sector. Most would agree that this division has worked well for our country. The government sector serves the public. That's why those who work for the government are called public servants. The for-profit sector serves its investors or stockholders. Those are the people who in the beginning put up the money to start the organization or joined in that support at a later time. The not-for-profit sector serves a mission or a purpose. Some think that this not-for-profit title is unfortunate because it defines us not by what we are, but by what we are not. So while "for-the-mission" sector sounds a bit awkward, even confusing, it is a truer definition of the not-for-profit sector.

All the sectors are regulated by the government. The government itself is regulated by its own constitution, by legislation, and by the checks and balances built in among the Administration (the President), the Legislature (the Congress), and the Judiciary (various courts including the Supreme Court). The for-profit sector is regulated by the government with rules about employment, profits, taxes, trade, and more. The not-for-profit sector also has government regulations, mostly about the use of funds, employment practices, and taxes. At its best, the government is in the business of seeing that not-for-profits are appropriately responsible to their missions, for-profits are appropriately responsible to their investors, and government is appropriately responsible to its Constitution and Bill of Rights.

We all know about and read about how things go wrong. How government sometimes falls into serving its own good rather than the public good, and how for-profits sometimes fall into serving their investors to the detriment of the public. The not-for-profit failing is most often connected to raising funds or using funds for the good of some individual or individuals rather than the advancement of the mission. In short, while the three-sector system may be one of the best yet devised, it, like all systems, can go awry. The job of the board in the not-for-profit sector is to see that that does not happen. The job is to be trustworthy about the mission—to see that all of the organization's activity and all of its funds are directed toward that mission.

There has been some confusion about the term "not-for-profit." Some people think that term is different than "nonprofit." Not so. The latter is sometimes used as shorthand for the former, but the terms are identical in meaning. We prefer not-for-profit, even though it is a definition of what an organization is not, because nonprofit seems to imply that an attitude of "well, we tried, but we are still without a profit" exists within the organization.

Not-for-profit organizations can indeed make money on their activities. It is legal and even good to make money on the services you provide, the admission to your events, or the courses you teach. The key is that all that money made (sometimes called earned income) must be put back into the budget to further the mission of the organization. It is also proper and good to have a budget balance at the end of the year. Again, that balance must go to next year's activities in service of the mission or to endowment in service of the future mission.

PAYING ATTENTION TO RULES AND REPORTS

There are a few forms and reports that must be submitted on a regular basis. One such form is the IRS Form 990—a summary of income and expenses for a given year, together with a report on the organization's core activity. This report is made to the Internal Revenue Service and is due annually on the fifteenth day of the fifth month after the end of the organization's fiscal year (typically either May 15 or November 15). You may, because of special circumstances, receive an extension until July 15 or January 15, depending on your budget year. It is also good to note that this form only has to be filed if the organization has incurred gross receipts of over $25,000.

Filing quarterly tax withholding statements may also be required if you have paid staff from whose salary federal tax is withheld. These reports are officially called IRS Form 941 and are due at the end of April, July, October, and January. In addition, some states require a quarterly report of salaries and contributions to unemployment compensation, as well as a semi-annual report of contributions to workers' compensation.

If you have staff that are receiving retirement benefits of any kind you will need to submit Form 5500 to the Internal Revenue Service. This report, calculated for the calendar year of contributions, should be submitted by July 31. While all this and what follows is correct as of this publication date, things change frequently at the IRS. You may want to check with an accountant.

What follows is a typical yearly calendar listing required reports as well as a few other suggested tasks that most organizations put on their annual calendar. In this example, we assume your budget year is the same as the calendar year.

A typical year of government reports and organizational administration

	Required	Suggested
JANUARY	Withholding tax payment*; W-2 forms to paid employees;1099-M forms to contracted personnel; Report employee income to state and local treasurers; Form 941**	
FEBRUARY		Begin audit of previous year's program and financial activity
MARCH	unemployment contribution report***	
APRIL	Form 941**	Report previous year's financial activity
MAY	IRS Form 990 (if fiscal year ends in December)	
JUNE	Workers' compensation contribution report****; unemployment report***	
JULY	Form 941**; Form 5500	
AUGUST		
SEPTEMBER	unemployment report***	
OCTOBER	Form 941**	Initiate budget building
NOVEMBER	IRS Form 990 (if fiscal year ends in July)	Conclude budget-building activity
DECEMBER	Workers' compensation report****; unemployment report***	Board approves annual budget for following year

* For most organizations, withholding payments are due each month. If your organization's payment is less than $2,500 per quarter, they are due quarterly. With larger organizations, withholding payments are due each payroll.

** Federal tax withholding reports due quarterly

*** Unemployment contribution reports due quarterly

**** Workers' compensation contribution reports due bi-annually

ABOUT LIABILITY

We have found that there are two main liability issues to avoid. The first is to avoid being frightened into purchasing a very expensive liability insurance policy for the board until you know the facts (like what your state laws say) and until you carefully calculate your risk. Secondly, do not assume that you as board members have no risk at all. Do not assume that only the organization is at risk of having to defend itself and/or pay restitution if someone sues your organization because they fell coming up your front steps or because they suffered additional trauma as a result of advice given by your counselors.

Here are the basics that you need to know:

1. If your organization participates in illegal activities and board members are involved in the wrongdoing, those members will likely be held personally liable.

2. Board members are also likely to be personally liable if the organization sets up a separate operation and then fails to keep the financial records of the two entities separate and identifiable.

3. Board members may be personally liable if they fail to exercise reasonable oversight of organizational activities that end up causing harm to someone, such as if board members allowed an employee with known drug or alcohol addiction to transport clients.

4. Liability protection generally comes in one of two forms:
   a. the bylaws of the organization provide for indemnification or protection against liability;
   b. the organization purchases directors and officers liability insurance.

Your state attorney general's office can provide you with the most up-to-date information on this important matter. The following is a summary of five guidelines concerning liability we suggest you review as a board. They are based upon information from a detailed description in *Governing Boards* by Cyril Houle.

1. Most states provide for the indemnification (protection) of board members. You should check the exact provision in this regard under the laws of your state.

2. State laws that apply to not-for-profit corporations provide guidelines concerning actions permissible on the part of boards. Some board member should be aware of these provisions and be prepared to monitor their application.

3. The board should make a conscious decision about how much directors' and officers' insurance it needs, what sort, and how much it is willing to pay.

4. Boards must exercise care in protecting themselves against board actions that might lead to fiscal liability. Pay particular attention to self-interested decisions, payroll taxes, and fraud, and deal with them quickly and forthrightly. Also of importance are problems related to mismanagement, dereliction of duty, and the offering of impermissible programs.

5. The board should establish checks on performance and reporting procedures that will likely reveal early detection of troubling issues.

If this all seems too complicated or burdensome, seek the advice of someone in your state attorney general's office or consult a trusted attorney.

RECORDS

All boards need to keep good records of their meetings, particularly noting any decisions made and who was in attendance. Usually that is the job of the board secretary, but anyone can record the meeting's proceedings—a volunteer, a part-time staff person, or a full-time administrative assistant. The advantage to using a non-board member is that it frees the secretary (who is a board member) to participate fully in the discussions at the board meeting. Make sure, though, that the board secretary checks the validity of the minutes, sees that they are submitted for board amendment and approval, and then keeps an official record in some way at least as substantial as a three-ring notebook.

From time to time, new organizational policies may emerge that are discussed and voted upon in the affirmative. These, of course, need to be recorded in the minutes. However, if they are only recorded in the minutes, they are very likely to get lost. Consider keeping a separate policy book and enter new policies as they are approved. Doing so will allow easy access, which is important since policies are second only to by-laws in guiding the conduct of an organization.

Finally, with any luck at all you have someone on your board or group of volunteers who loves history. Too many organizations fail to retain in any orderly fashion all those pictures, clippings, invitations, and programs that will prove so very important in keeping an accurate and colorful account of the history of the organization. Designate that one person be in charge of keeping in one safe place everything on paper that the organization produces. This is often called an archive, but whatever you wish to call it, it is good material to have organized and easy to find as you talk to new board members and prospective funders, or try to celebrate your 10th or 50th anniversary as an organization.

Section III

Leadership
of the Board

Chapter 14

The Board President
as Leader

I f you are the board president and there is no executive director
or staff, you have one set of challenges. If, on the other hand,
you do have an executive, there is another set of challenges. This
second set will be discussed in the next chapter. For now we want
to address you as a leader, and we want you to start seriously
thinking of yourself as a leader.

"I'm just managing" is a curious phrase in human interchange
usually uttered in response to "How are you doing today?" "Just managing" means getting by, going through the motions, taking things as they
come. That kind of managing is not what you want to be doing as board
president. Being a manager, making sure things are done correctly and
on time is not a big enough role for you as president. Someone does
need to do that. There is, after all, nothing wrong with managers. Every
organization needs them. However, it is possible that the problems in the
life of organizations today exist not because we do not have managers,
but because we do not have leaders. We ask you to consider being a
leader. Actually, we ask you to decide, to choose to be a leader by making
your own distinctive mark on the life and mission of your organization.

Warren Bennis, a notable writer on leadership, lists the distinctions
between leaders and managers this way:

- The manager administers; the leader innovates.
- The manager maintains; the leader develops.
- The manager has a short-range view; the leader has a
  long-range perspective.
- The manager asks how and when; the leader asks what and why.
- The manager is a copy; the leader is an original.

Original is good and original you are. You may not be Susan B.
Anthony giving a lifetime to securing the right of women to vote. You
may not be Winston Churchill calling for great courage in dark times.
You may not be Martin Luther King, Jr. powerfully claiming that we

could do far better as a nation. But you, like they, have a distinctive self, a special voice and therefore a unique way of expressing leadership. Their way of leading had integrity. Their speaking and their acting as leaders followed naturally out of who they were as people. They found their way and their distinctive leadership expression had great power to do good things.

We urge you to discover a sense of your own distinctive abilities to do good and necessary things while you are board president. Of course you must pay attention to income, expenses, structures, processes, and order, not disregarding the special challenges your organization may be facing during your tenure. But do more and do it in a way that is more representative of who you are as a person and a leader.

What might that be? Before giving you some examples of presidents acting on their own special gifts, think through these questions and talk them over with the board:

- What is it about this organization that first drew me to it?
- What is there about me that relates most strongly to the mission of this place?
- What is there that I care most deeply about that can be connected most usefully to what this organization now needs?
- For what aspects of the life of this organization do I wish to take responsibility?
- As board president, what worthy mark do I wish to leave on this place? For what do I wish to be remembered?

These questions may move you closer to discovering your own distinctive way of leading. Here are two examples that may help you as well. Each is a brief account of how a particular board president expressed his or her particular "thing" in a way that made a significant positive impact on their organizations.

Yolanda was an artist with a great sense of color, spirit, and beauty that infected her whole life. She also loved children and cared deeply about their well-being, which is why she agreed to be on the board of Neighborhood Day Care, and largely why she soon emerged as a natural leader and was elected president. Not surprisingly, money and particularly salaries were always a problem, and during her two-year term of office she dedicated herself to addressing that issue in a variety of ways. In fact, after two years Neighborhood Day Care's teachers and assistants were the best paid in town, and, what's more, that accomplishment was achieved with a balanced budget. For that, Yolanda would always be remembered and appreciated, especially by the staff. But the big thing she did that grew directly out of who she was and what she cared about was to change the aesthetic environment of the whole building.

It was drab with too few windows and too many off-white to gray walls. The classrooms were colorful enough with the children's art and bright books and toys, but the lobby, offices and halls were like February. If a president with artistic spirit did not make a difference here, who would? She mobilized parents to paint and art collectors and artists to loan bright landscapes and colorful still lifes. An instant gallery arose. The whole environment of the organization changed from February to May and a very powerful and lasting imprint had been made by a board president. Yolanda did a very simple thing: she led in a way natural for her and in a direction that matched an organizational need. Yet she did not forget about doing business at the same time.

Ralph worked with personnel issues as part of his job in a small-size company. He was full of a good, kind-hearted spirit that made people want to be around him. He first joined the board of the Leukemia Foundation because one of his favorite nieces had been diagnosed with that dreaded disease when she was nine. He felt helpless to do much for her but thought this was one thing he could do for the cause. On the board he helped with special events rather than work on personnel issues as he did during the rest of the week. He really didn't think of himself as a leader, but he was so well liked and trusted that after four years he was asked to serve as the board president.

While assisting with special events, he discovered that too many people in the community didn't know about leukemia and very few realized there was a local foundation. Ralph knew instinctively that part of being a good president was taking care of the basics like (in this case) public relations. Though he didn't know much about public relations, he organized a board committee that included outside professionals to address the relative invisibility of the organization. Quickly, the work of the public relations committee paid off, and everyone appreciated this new initiative. Ralph was tending to business.

But the real thing that changed in the life of that organization during the time Ralph was president was that a close, almost family-like community was created. Ralph spent significant time with each board member, in addition to the three staff people as well. He listened, he expressed understanding, and he exhibited a regard and kindness for those people that changed the culture of the place. He began each board meeting with personal stories about what had been happening in the lives of board members. Birthday cards magically appeared and announcements were made about special awards and promotions. That was Ralph in action: a warm and generous human being practicing the presidency in a way that reflected his warmth and generosity. That organization will never be the same because of that president's willingness to exercise his own distinctive gifts in that setting, all the while taking care of the public relations requirements of the agency.

These are examples of board presidents being presidential in ways that are natural to them—board presidents leading, not merely managing. We hope you find some of the same excitement and satisfaction wherever or whenever you practice board leadership.

Chapter 15

Leading Together:
The Board and the Executive

I f you don't have an executive director, most of what follows may not be for you. On the other hand, there are some charts included in this chapter about "who does what" that may be useful as you organize the work of your board.

Let's begin with a rather big challenge. Our experience is, unfortunately, that boards and executives sometimes begin to behave as adversaries rather than colleagues. It is critical to address the "who does what and why" questions as they relate to both board and executive so that you can work more as a team.

First, we urge you to create your own way of working together. The extra emphasis here should be on "own." It is your working relationship, your organization; you know best its particular character and, more so, what you as a responsible leader want for it. Resist advice that begins "boards should always..." or "executives ought never..." There are only a few "always" and "nevers" in the world of organizational life, because there are so many special cases—special people forging working relationships in ways that work best for them. You need to decide what will be your predominant way of working as board president with the executive in your organization.

Generally speaking, boards and executives tend to operate in one of four ways. While these ways are not entirely distinct from one another, for purposes of discussion and decision about how you wish to operate, here they are in brief:

1. Board initiates and decides, executive receives and implements.

This is probably the most formal way of running an organization. The board is strong, well in control, and the executive is clear about professional activity based on board directives. This tends to work well when board members are designated representatives from other organizations or control the funding sources. In this model, executives do well who are good at faithfully carrying out the decisions made by the board.

2. Executive proposes, board disposes.

The executive takes the lead in developing new ideas, programs, and funding. The board critiques, amends, and decides. Board activity is focused on review and response with the executive acting as initiator. At best, a fine balance is reached between executive creativity and board control. At worst, the executive ends up lobbying ideas and the organization moves toward an adversarial mode with innovation and creativity on one side and practicality and control on the other.

3. Executive acts, board is informed and consulted.

Small organizations, or those fashioned around the abilities of a strong leader, often function in this manner. The board acts as consultant as needed and the executive stays in the lead with the ideas and their execution. If the paid leadership is consistent in consulting the board and the board is willing to have a more passive role, this can work well. If the executive fails to consult or makes decisions or takes action that embarrasses the board, it does not work well.

4. Board and executive jointly initiate and implement.

This operates best where boards are willing to share power and executives are willing to share programs. Most people think that boards set policy, not executives; and that executives must design and run programs, not boards. While this mode of operation is not without merit, it does tend to keep both board and executive from being flexible enough to use the rich variety of knowledge and ability that exists in the leadership of an organization.

For instance, most organizations have boards and executives with a mix of creativity and practicality, policy-making and program development skills. Effective organizations find ways of using this variety of abilities without being confined by strict role definitions. However, this joint initiation and implementation process does not work well where the executive or board members, for whatever reason, want well defined and protected roles.

There are, of course, a near infinite number of ways to run an organization. Your own way may be a mix of the above or something quite different. The four presented are simply a starting point for discussions about partnership building between the board and executive presently responsible for the life of the organization.

The following chart may help you to think clearly about how you want your partnership to work. Begin by using a separate form for each category of the following recommended categories. (You may have others.)

- Mission and Purposes
- Program and Services
- Marketing and Public Relations
- Planning and Evaluation
- Funding and Finance
- Administration and Staffing

Second, check opposite the Leadership Function the primary party who will carry out that function. In some cases you may decide that a particular function may occur in two or more places. You might want to have board members and the executive fill out the forms separately, then discuss them and work toward a consensus. In either case, you may want to put yourself in an experimental frame of mind in order to try out a new way for a year, then decide how well it works.

Deciding Who Has the Responsibility

Organizational function _____

Leadership Function	Executive	Board President	Committee Chair	Board Committee	Full Board
Initiate	❏	❏	❏	❏	❏
Formulate	❏	❏	❏	❏	❏
Propose	❏	❏	❏	❏	❏
Decide	❏	❏	❏	❏	❏
Implement	❏	❏	❏	❏	❏
Monitor	❏	❏	❏	❏	❏
Evaluate	❏	❏	❏	❏	❏
Reformulate	❏	❏	❏	❏	❏

Note: In some cases more than one person or group may have the responsibility. If so, check two or more places.

One more way to help the board-executive team work well together is for the board president to have a one-on-one conversation with the executive. We suggest the following four different conversations that stand out in our minds as having been particularly rewarding.

1. A conversation about goals

Try a conversation about the goals you have for your term of office. You bring to this role different qualities than the previous board president. We urge you not to shy away from leaving your own special mark, your own unique influence on the organization. That might be a broader funding base, a new and stronger relationship with the media, the extension of a program to a new audience, or something else.

2. A conversation about environment

Try another conversation about the kind of environment the two of you want to create. Maybe it includes the permission to ask more questions, to inquire and even challenge reports and proposals. Or maybe you wish to ensure that more time is spent on big issues and less energy given over to small details. Perhaps the promptness of beginnings and endings of meetings, and maneuvering through an efficient agenda is what you want. Whatever the special environmental condition you wish to bring about, merely announcing it won't make it happen. The two of you need to embody it, model it for the rest of the leaders, and see that it happens in practice.

3. A conversation about what to avoid

Try a conversation about what you want to avoid—not big obvious things like "misunderstandings," but more specific things like private conversations in board meetings while business is being conducted, or surprising the other with a new proposal in a board meeting. You may also want to avoid having too-full agendas, re-discussing and re-deciding an issue, allowing any one or two board members to dominate a discussion, or creating a structure and practice by which the executive committee becomes the in-group, the quasi-board. You no doubt will have your own favorite list of things you don't want to happen.

4. A conversation about board meeting preparation

Try yet another conversation about all the issues that surround board meetings, the before, during, and after tasks that one or the other of you will inherit. Following is a list of some examples that executives and board presidents divide in different ways:

1. Writing the meeting announcement reminder
2. Telephoning special people to get them there
3. Seeing that minutes are ready for presentation
4. Creating the agenda
5. Writing the agenda for distribution
6. Arranging the meeting space
7. Arranging the refreshments, if any
8. Making sure minutes are taken and checked
9. Thanking special guests
10. Inquiring about members not present

Though these are small items, they absolutely contribute to well-run meetings, and can so easily fall unattended between the two of you if not discussed.

The focus of this chapter has been on getting your partnership with the executive off to a good start. A "good start" means that:

1. your partnership is uniquely yours, designed for your special situation;

2. there is clarity between the two of you about who is responsible for the various organizational functions during your time of office; and

3. the executive-board president relationship is attended to, respected, and fits with the character and tone of the whole organization.

Chapter 16

Executive Evaluation

E valuation of the executive is a task that you as a board member need to see is done fairly and well, which means at least two things. First, the executive should have the opportunity to do a self-assessment as well as receive your assessment. Second, you as a board member need to make sure the whole experience is one in which your executive learns and grows, rather than feels only rated or judged. The most important reason to do regular evaluations of executives is to provide them with information and opinions from a variety of people who care enough about them and the organization to help them grow and develop.

There are many ways to go about the task of executive evaluation. We have collected four for your review and utilization: Rating Key Performance Areas, Examining Crucial Relationships, Contracting for Effectiveness, and Assessing for Personal Satisfaction. You may want to combine two or more, or you may want to try one way one year and another way the next year.

1. Rating key performance areas

Name of executive: _____

Name/Relationship of rater: _____

Date of individual rating: _____

Date of joint review: _____

Instructions: Place an "E" in the appropriate column if you are the executive doing a self-rating. Board members utilizing a separate copy of the form might wish to place a check in the column that most nearly reflects their evaluation of performance on the component. Add comments that provide rationale for the rating and/ or offer recommendations for improvement. Determine relative importance of each category for your organization.

	Excellent	Very Good	Good	Poor	Very Poor
1. Agency/operation planning					
• Understands mechanisms of strategic planning process					
• Able to analyze areas of responsibility, both short and long term					
Comments:					
2. Implementation of strategic plan					
• Able to successfully deliver plan and react positively to anticipated problems in order to meet or surpass plan					
Comments:					
3. Financial management					
• Understands and can properly apply analytical skills					
• Able to analyze and control expenses and enhance revenues					
• Delivers budget goal at year-end					
Comments:					

	Excellent	Very Good	Good	Poor	Very Poor
4. Systems management					
• Understands and can develop and use systems and information					
• Properly uses all available resources to achieve maximum performance					
Comments:					
5. Staff management/development					
• Effectively recruits and selects staff					
• Effectively trains and develops staff					
• Maintains effective staff relations in areas of responsibility					
• Minimizes staff turnover					
Comments:					
6. Program management/delivery					
• Effectively orients participants to overall program					
• Effectively trains and develops participants					
• Successfully coordinates and schedules the program					
• Develops and utilizes useful evaluative procedures with participants concerning program, staff, and self-development					
• Appropriately assists in resolving problems:					
– between and among clients					
– between and among staff and clients					
– of clients concerning program					
Comments:					

	Excellent	Very Good	Good	Poor	Very Poor
7. Personal management skills					
• Manages work to meet deadlines					
• Completes work accurately					
• Delegates effectively					
• Takes proper action on own initiative					
Comments:					
8. Priorities/areas of responsibility					
• Effectively sets priorities and apportions time among agency/ program administration, staff supervision, and program delivery					
Comments:					
9. Communication/reporting skills					
• Capable of explaining and marketing the organizational goals, processes and results					
• Appropriately and effectively communicates with:					
– board members					
– staff					
– clients					
– community leaders					
Comments:					

Final comments and signatures:

Topics and issues around which there were discrepancies between executive and rater perceptions:

Conclusions/agreements/disagreements resulting from joint review(s):

Signatures:

_____   _____
Executive   Date

_____   _____
Board representative   Date

_____   _____
Board representative or other appointed person   Date

Note: The above is a minor adaptation of a form created by the Center for New Directions, Columbus, Ohio. We thank them.

2. The next form, **Examining Crucial Relationships,** analyzes how well the executive relates to the primary individuals and groupings of individuals inside and outside the organization. It is organized as a chart with questions about each of these relationships. These relationships are discussed in conversations between the board chair and the executive or a personnel committee and the executive. The questions are the same for each of the relationships.

Ask each question about each of the key relationships:

1. How has it been effective in the past?

2. What needs more effort and development?

3. What are the sources of resistance and reinforcement that need attention?

Examining Crucial Relationships of the Executive Director

Relationships	Satisfactory effectiveness	Needs development	Comments
1. Board			
2. Board chair			
3. Board committee			
4. Committee chairs			
5. Staff			
6. Colleague institutions			
7. Community leaders			
8. Funders			

3. **Contracting for effectiveness** aims at creating a short-term agreement or contract on two or three goals in each of several areas. This type of evaluation requires ability in negotiating and goal-setting and is based on the assumption that identifying and achieving attainable goals increases the likelihood of effectiveness.

Periodically over the course of one year, the executive director meets with the board chair (and whoever else is designated) to produce a brief, one-page document listing no more than four goals agreed upon by both. The emphasis should be on making things happen. Therefore goals that have a high likelihood of being accomplished should be set.

Some of the areas for which goals might be written include:

- professional growth or career development goals (for example, achieve a specialization in marketing)

- skill development goals (for example, learn a new computer program)

- organizational mission goals (for example, develop better media relations)

- communication or relational goals (for example, meet with each board member separately once during the year)

- strategy, process, or structure goals (for example, develop a new personnel manual)

In using this approach, it is important to take time for reflective conversation and to reinforce positive results. The more people feel they can succeed, the more likely they are to try new things. The approach should be one of focusing on the achievable rather than identifying goals that have little or no chance of being attained.

4. The fourth example, **assessing personal satisfaction,** is a list of questions not usually included on traditional evaluations. These questions relate to the fact that in one way or another your organization is in the "life satisfaction" business. That is, you want people to have better and more satisfied lives as a result of the service or product your organization provides.

Likewise, you want to have an executive director who is also having a personally satisfying work experience. In the end, you hope that your organization will have a positive impact on the lives of those who come in contact with it. That would certainly include the executive who directs it. Here are some questions to provoke a thoughtful conversation concerning personal satisfaction:

1. How does this organization impact the rest of your life?

2. How would your life be different if you were not part of this organization?

3. What specifically would you change to make your experience in the organization more satisfying?

4. What about this organization makes you proud?

Keep in mind that a personally healthy and satisfied executive may be one of the best testimonies to the real effectiveness of the organization in making a positive impact on the community.

Chapter 17

Executive Succession
and Search

This chapter may be skipped if the organization you serve does not have an executive. If you do have an executive, what follows should help you plan for what happens when that person leaves. Whenever they do and for whatever reason, the conversation about leaving, searching, and starting anew is a good one to have. In what follows we will share with you some pieces of that conversation that we have found to be helpful.

Regardless of the amount of leadership you as a board have shared with your executive in the past, now, at this critical time of executive transition, is when you must take the lead. This may require a retreat or outside consultation, and it certainly will require extra time and renewed commitment to the life and mission of your organization. You will not want to exclude your executive, but you will want to make it clear that leadership for the transition process is yours. You are the ones who will remain and be entrusted with the organization's life and mission. You are the ones therefore who must take charge and assume full responsibility for the well-being of the organization.

It has been our experience that organizations that have relatively successful transitions have boards that take strong and thoughtful leadership in five areas. Your organization's unique situation will determine which of them will be most important. All five areas are worthy of your review.

1. Planning

You may have anywhere from three to eighteen months as a transition period. You must plan wisely from the time you find that your executive is leaving until the actual departure. In the best situation, your plan for the transitional period would be embedded in a two- to three-year plan for the organization. Here's an example of a scenario that seemed to work well: Upon hearing that the executive would leave in nine to twelve months, the board appointed a planning committee to develop a comprehensive plan for all aspects of the organization that included the time period of the transition and one year beyond. This approach placed the activity of the transition in the broader context of an ongoing plan for the life of the organization. It was helpful in that it did not isolate the transition period from the important work to follow, and it was useful in providing fresh information about the direction of the organization for prospective candidates for the executive position.

This plan involved special attention to capturing the existing culture of the organization. Lively board and staff conversations about "who we are and what we wish to preserve" enabled the board to broaden and deepen its understanding and therefore to better exert the necessary leadership. These conversations were useful to the existing director ("They do know what we are all about") and useful as well to the prospective candidates who inquired about the special personality of the organization.

2. Transition purposes

There are some obvious and unavoidable things that need to be done during the transition that relate to honoring the departing executive and searching for the new one. It is important for the transition period to have a purpose that goes beyond these necessary tasks of search and celebration. For example, one organization consolidated two of its programs into one to save time and resources. Another sought and received funds to initiate a new program for teenage youth, an audience not previously served. Another added additional staff meetings to do training that broadened the scope of what each staff member knew and could do. Still another spent six months re-working and renewing one of its basic programs.

The point of all this is to keep the organization alive and developing during the transition. The work of transition is important work but must not be allowed to be the only, certainly not the primary, work that the organization does. It seems that transition as a whole works better when it does not consume all the creative energies of the organization. Organizational programs, processes, staffing, and systems cannot be permitted to be dormant during an extended succession transition. The work of the organization must continue.

3. The search

What follows are a few basics that are important aspects of an effective search process.

Think about representation. For most organizations, having a search committee of five to nine members is about right. Such a compact number dictates careful thinking about who those few are. Apart from obvious age, gender, and race considerations, you should consider selecting people who represent different aspects of the organization (programming, marketing, fundraising), new and seasoned board members, those with different points of view, formal and informal leaders, and those with previous search experience as well as some who are fresh to the task.

Be clear about the charge. What are the guidelines and givens that the board has established? Now is the time to know (or ask) and be particularly clear about:

- a preliminary job description
- the salary range
- the benefit package
- the committee's budget and expenses
- the geographical scope of the search
- acceptability of "inside" candidates
- preferred date for the new executive to begin
- particular skills or traits deemed as important from the organization's assessment
- the use of a search consultant
- whether one or multiple candidates are to be recommended and slated for board review
- process and responsibility for final selection
- the point at which the committee completes its work

Begin with your own valuable experience. Some of you may have previously chosen executives. You already have ideas about what you are looking for and how to go about getting it. Think about your interaction with other organizational executives. Who are the best you have known? Which of their actions and attitudes earned your respect? What conclusions have you drawn about effective leaders from those experiences? Narrow your conclusions from sentences to words or phrases. What are the five or ten words that best describe what you think is important in an executive?

Now, be negative. Most of us have had bad experiences as well, and are quite sure of things we want to avoid. Again, spare the long story in favor of the phrase. Be clear about traits you dislike. Perhaps you can finish a sentence like "I don't want to select someone who is _____" or "Executives I find most difficult are those who _____."

Create a pool of diverse candidates. You must do this if you are going to draw attractive candidates, including those who may not be actively on the job market. The position needs to be advertised and discussed through all the informal networks of colleagues, professional associations, past board members, funders, and community institutions. Have an open discussion in the committee about gender, race, and age. This is not "what does the law require" (although that is worth discussing), but what does the mix of values and organizational requirements suggest? What do you care about? What do you want to make sure you communicate about yourselves by this process? The search committee must pursue a diversity of sources in order to assure a rich mix of fine candidates.

Develop an application. What do you want to know before deciding to meet this candidate? Many standard applications are available to review, and since the business of writing resumes is thriving, you no doubt will receive plenty. Many candidates show skill in resume writing far beyond skill in leadership. Often, our experience is that because of many factors (such as long application forms and dazzling resumes), searchers end up with non-crucial information not easily comparable from candidate to candidate. You probably can't avoid the resume rush, but you can devise a simple required application to give you information to compare.

Three categories of questions that we have found to be of particular value are:

1. questions that get at the candidate's degree of self-assessment and reflection,
2. questions that probe the candidate's way of working, and
3. questions that point toward the candidate's sense of your mission.

Example questions for each category follow.

- *Self-reflection and assessment*

What are your strengths as a leader and what skills are you still developing? What would your present board say about your leadership ability and style?

- *Way of working*

If you are already an executive, describe how you work with your board president and board. How often would you have staff meetings and what would be the chief purposes of those sessions?

- *Sense of mission*

How would you describe the mission of our organization? What aspects of our mission and program would you be most likely to adjust or change? Why?

4. Stability

While there is not one best way to run an organization, a transition period presents a good time to get more clear and ordered around systems, structures, staffing, and financial stability. Many organizations run by a strong executive rely too much on the sheer will and energy of that executive. As a result things like systems, structures, and staffing are loose to informal. One organization decided that the transition was a good time to rewrite position descriptions as a way of better clarifying the work of the staff. Another organization reworked the structure and responsibility of board committees and chairs. Another involved an enlarged fund development committee in reviewing and assessing all the sources of funding and deciding on some new strategies that included a greater number of board members.

Just as a time of transition is a time to continue to do the creative work of the organization, it is also a time to clarify, organize, and sharpen the systems and procedures that keep the organization fit. This stabilization process is important work in and of itself because it lays important groundwork for the new executive leadership.

5. Rituals

You may want to create rituals or celebrations as part of the transition process. The board needs to determine what is a natural fit for the organization—the degree of formality and fun, the extent to which the personal and professional will be merged. Begin by considering who it is that needs to say goodbye to the director in a celebratory way. Depending on the size of the town and how public a figure your executive has been, it could be that you go beyond the board and close constituents to the broader community. When and if that seems like the right way to proceed, you may then have to create another setting in which the "immediate family" of the organization has the chance to honor the executive in a more personal way. Again, it is for you to decide what works best in your situation—what is the best mix of celebration and tribute, of written and oral communications, of mementos and gifts. The transition marks a major passage for your organization and it will likely feel more completed and concluded if you pay attention to some rituals in which those important to your organization can participate.

Chapter 18

The Gathering of the Leadership: Designing Board Meetings

P lease don't skip this chapter. If you happen to be a board president, vice-president, president-elect or for that matter any board member who keeps hoping for board meetings that both engage and produce, this section is for you.

Imagine all it takes to do a special event: thinking about the focus of the activity, structuring the time so that the movement from one thing to the next seems effortless, tending to all the details of space, and determining what people sip and where they sit. With that special event picture in mind, we'd like you to think about your board meetings as requiring a similar level of thorough planning—thoughtful consideration of the order of things and careful attention to detail.

We most wish to convey that you have very few hours in a year when you have the leadership of your organization together in one place. This "gathering of the leadership" to exercise tender loving care over the life of your organization is in fact a very special event that deserves much attention and planning. We offer three aspects for your consideration here and for future discussion with your executive: creating the agenda, sharing the responsibility, and progressing through the meeting.

CREATING THE AGENDA

One board president we know meets with the executive two weeks before the board meeting to review how the previous meeting went and to form the agenda for the next. The advantage of the two weeks time frame is that it is close enough that most of the issues will be apparent by then and far enough in advance that there is still time to send board members the completed agenda via mail or even e-mail. This pair has also over the months come to agree on a few general notions about the agenda. One such notion is that every meeting has at least one hefty issue that requires the board to use its imagination and exercise its discussion skills. In so doing, there is a far better chance that members will come away feeling the meeting was, in fact, significant. Too often agendas are too long and full of minor issues and matters of strategy and logistics.

Boards need the experience of being led to the bigger, overarching issues that command their minds and their creative energies. One child-serving agency we know asked its board to grapple with the issues of the danger of dependency on a single funding source. Another agency serving teenagers started by discussing recent research on the impact of television on behavior.

Actually, it's not a bad idea to start board meetings with these kinds of issues. Meetings have a way of finding a level of significance early on. So if you begin with the small items you are more likely to have a small-stuff kind of meeting. Whereas beginning with the big issues sets a tone of importance and depth that will, with any luck, permeate the whole meeting.

Ending well is also a good thing. We know of one mental health board that always ends with "good news from around the town." We find this to be a nice and memorable way to end a meeting—hearing five or six things to make you proud. We know of another board of a drug treatment agency that ends with personal letters from clients, news clippings, and announcements about recognitions and awards received by board and staff members. This approach makes for a positive and upbeat state of mind as you depart the board meeting.

Sometimes board members complain that they are never quite sure what is expected of them on a specific agenda item. It usually goes something like this, "So do you want to hear what I think, want me to just nod my head yes or no, or just let you know I heard what was reported?" A board of a historical society handles it this way. They organize the agenda into three broad categories: Items for Discussion and Decision, Items for Ratification, and Items for Information. The items are placed in that particular order to ensure that the bigger issues are addressed first. Then it is always clear what is being asked. Try organizing the agenda items so that it is clear what is expected of the board.

SHARING RESPONSIBILITY
FOR AGENDA ITEMS

There is one final matter the board president may wish to clarify before the board members are in the room. Each board president-executive partnership develops its own way of making the board meetings work well. While there are some general guidelines, the specifics should be decided in a way that works for the two of you.

Though the traditional expectation is that the president formally conducts the meeting by proceeding through the agenda, in some not-for-profit organizations the board president simply opens or closes the meeting, which is run by the executive director.

Identify those agenda items that either the board president or the executive will always handle. For example, you might decide that the president will always present, modify, and proceed through the agenda and that the executive director will always be responsible for the staff report (written or verbal).

Other items could vary. You could decide that, at budget time, it is more appropriate for the executive director to explain the proposed budget. But if the budget contains new salary increases, for instance, the board president may choose to present the information. If the organization has a finance director, then the presentation obviously could be delegated to that person.

There are some matters for which both of you will probably want to assume joint (or equal) responsibility. Ensuring that the board meeting begins and ends on time is one of our favorite examples.

The key to having a successful board meeting is that, acting in partnership with the executive, you identify aspects of the leadership of the meeting for which each is best suited. We hope that both of you will consider the benefits of a shared, team approach to leading meetings and, through thoughtful planning, will balance your leadership styles, gifts, and actions to achieve efficiency and harmony.

You may wish to make use of the following checklist to determine your own special design for the leadership of the board meeting.

The Balancing Act of Leading Board Meetings

You decide who...	Board President	Executive Director	Both Share
Begins and ends board meeting on time.			
Welcomes group; makes everyone feel at ease.			
Guides last-minute changes.			
Draws out knowledge and resources of board members.			
Gives staff reports and updated information.			
Proceeds through agenda.			
Modifies agenda.			
Restates each item and brings discussion to closure.			
Summarizes progress.			
Assigns action items to appropriate people.			
Encourages interaction; draws out quiet people.			
Applauds volunteer efforts, thanks group, celebrates achievements.			
Add your own: _____ _____ _____			

THE MEETING IN PROGRESS

Robert's Rules of Order

Worth knowing and especially worth following for complex and controversial issues, Robert's Rules of Order have survived the test of time and practice. In case you are not quite familiar, here is a greatly condensed version that summarizes most of what you need to know. This we borrowed from Brian O'Connell, for years the executive director of The Independent Sector. In his *The Board Member's Book*, this appears in a chapter aptly titled "Robert's Rules of Order—Demystified."

Starting at the most elementary level, this is the way a group formally makes a decision:

- One of the members will move that a decision be made (this is proposing that the board go on record in favor of a certain definite action).

- Another member of the group will second the motion, which means "support" for the action proposed. (The second is necessary to be certain that the issue is of interest to more than one person.)

- Once the motion has been made and seconded, there is discussion, clarification, and debate.

- When the subject has been covered fully, there is the vote.

- Prior to both discussion and vote, the person in the chair should restate the motion to be certain everyone knows what is being discussed and decided.

That should suffice for ninety percent of the business in most organizations. However, if you are a quasi-public institution or dealing with highly controversial issues with community-wide ramifications, a stricter use of Robert's Rules may become essential.

Aside from the use of Robert's Rules there are other process details worth considering to ensure an orderly meeting. Having struggled through (sometimes sailed through) more than a few (hundred) board meetings ourselves, here is a list of our own favorite things to note:

An effective meeting checklist

1. Being polite is a good thing at dinner, but at board meetings, if it means no disagreements are allowed, it's not such a good thing. Disagreements can be healthy, especially when done in an agreeable fashion.

2. Too much information on too many pages is confusing and can inhibit good, clear discussions.

3. Too little information will cause any thoughtful board member to put off a decision until all the necessary information is available.

4. Demonstrating that you are able to reach healthy consensus out of initial disagreement encourages board members to express divergent opinions.

5. See that everyone has the opportunity to express themselves by moderating those who tend to be dominant and assisting those who tend to be shy.

6. Decisions reached after lengthy or difficult debate should be acted upon promptly so that the effort is worth it all.

7. Don't reconsider decisions reached after long and thoughtful discussions unless significant new circumstances have arisen.

8. Respect everyone's time. Starting promptly discourages tardiness. Ending promptly encourages focused discussions (and will make you popular).

9. Have a clear and fast decision-making process in place and insist that everyone respects it and does not go around it.

10. Finally, practice discussing some medium-to-small issues in the following categories with the board so that when the big ones come along you will be experienced at dealing with them.
    - Practice making changes in program and administration.
    - Practice reviewing and assessing things.
    - Practice facing the controversial.

Section IV
The Board and the Community

Chapter 19

Leading Change and Renewal

It is almost always useful for the board to think and to ask, "How can we change and do better?" Some of this will happen during a planning process once a year. That may or may not be enough for your organization. You may wish to build such conversations about change into every other board meeting. What we want to do is list and comment on all the various aspects of your organization's programs and services that would probably benefit from review at least once or twice a year. In doing so you may decide that 90% of the items are just the way you would like them to be. But likely there will be a thing or two where some change in the planning or implementing will make it better. Making things better is one task boards ought to be doing. It may be one of your most important roles as leaders.

We offer here a list of the items common to most organizations. We do not presume to tell you what to do, but we do suggest that in these eight categories there are probably changes you may want to consider.

1. *The activity itself.* What do you offer? Sometimes a service or program you have been offering is no longer needed. If the popularity of a program greatly decreases, don't automatically assume that the best response is to produce more or different marketing. Even worse would be having the superior attitude: "People just don't know what's good for them anymore." Maybe the need for your service or program no longer exists, or maybe someone else is fulfilling it. What you can count on is that the times (needs, attitudes, competition) change and you must be flexible and creative enough to come up with a new program or service that responds to those changes and yet is still faithful to your mission.

2. *The audience.* For whom are you doing this? This can be a tough one. If one of your cherished programs has been for teenagers and all of a sudden the high school is doing the same thing during the school day, you probably will have to make a change. Or if the new countywide senior center starts offering for free what you did for $12—guess what

will happen to your audience? In most cases there are more than enough needs out there among the people in your area that you can adjust a bit (different age group, different socio-economic level, different number of years of education) and still do something worthy of your mission.

3. *The location.* Where is this all happening? Maybe twenty years ago you could offer everything you did in one location and people would gladly come to you, but probably not anymore. For a variety of good and not-so-good reasons, many people will not travel to the county seat once a week for whatever service your organization might offer. In a similar vein, many people think that programs offered in the basement of a church, community center, or bank building just aren't good enough or they would be held in a nicer place. We may not like it but where and in what kind of facility a program is offered has an impact on who and how many show up. If your current location isn't working, it's best to get over not liking it and get on to thinking about alternative locations and buildings.

4. *Scheduling.* When does all this happen? Some of us are finding that while only five or ten years ago people would come out at 7:30 p.m. on a weeknight for a program, now fewer and fewer will. They get home from work late and tired and they won't go back out. This is another one of those "times have changed and so must we." Only you can find out what times of the week and times of the day work best in your particular situation. You may even need to experiment a bit. Many are finding that while people would gladly attend a two and one-half hour program with intermission a few years ago, now a one and one-half hour program with no intermission works much better.

5. *Fees and admissions.* What does it cost? How many times do we hear that people pay $100 an hour for a therapy session but won't pay us $40 for (fill in the blank), or that people pay $35 for a country music concert but won't spend $10 for our (fill in the blank). This may be true, and if it is, the question your organization should be asking is what will we do about it? In a time of too many options, a variety of pricing options can be explored in order for your organization to succeed, including vouchers, gift certificates, family rates, scholarships, and discounts for multiple programs or services. Notice "free" was not listed as an option, since many people think that what is free isn't worth much. Designing new, creative ways of pricing is very important in most communities.

6. *Communications.* How do people find out about this? For sure, five years ago we wouldn't have sent out 100 invitations or announcements on a computer listserv. Maybe you shouldn't today, but it is one example of how communication has changed. You need to think about the right mix of direct mail, posters, T.V. ads, radio ads, newspaper ads, newspaper stories, or public service announcements that will work best for you in your community. Of course, do not overlook "organized" word of mouth, as in "bring a friend or neighbor." Many people still will only go places recommended by someone they trust or where someone they know will be in attendance to make them feel welcomed.

Also, pay attention to the look and tone of your printed materials. From time to time do a test with a variety of people. Do they think the piece looks too artsy, too cheap, too colorless, too silly…too what? Sometimes an otherwise worthwhile program can be undermined by the way it is written or the graphics and colors used to convey the message. In short, all the materials you send out and use should look like you, should have some consistent look. Beyond that, they can look one way or another depending on what particular event you are promoting and the people you wish to attract. Again, it is often best to get the fresh eyes of an outsider looking at and responding to how it is you portray yourself in printed materials.

7. *Personnel.* Who is going to run it? You may not have a lot of choice regarding personnel if there is a small staff or no staff at all, but don't give up on this one. You may wish to recruit three new volunteers to change how an activity is being perceived. Or you may wish to diversify the age group of those in charge, the racial backgrounds, or whether they are predominantly men or women. The issue of personnel is one in which new faces may be good just because they are new. There may be financial implications to consider. How many full-time people can you afford to assign, how many part-time or hourly people, and how many volunteers? There's a lot to think about, but the main point is to not assume that all the same people who have been running a particular program must continue to do so. That assumption is probably not good for the image of your organization and it may quickly tire out those dear people.

8. *Partnerships.* With whom might we do this? In the next chapter on community, we talk in some detail about this subject. Our experience with partnerships is that we probably spend too much time thinking about how to out-do or overcome the competition and not enough time thinking about how we might work together. Establishing partnerships creates a much nicer feeling in the community—knowing that those serving seniors are trying to figure out as many ways as they can to work together. Likewise, a positive public image is achieved when all those who offer various arts activities and performances organize to do joint presentations. More often than not, these partnerships benefit the people you serve. The services are better and more diverse, the performances have greater variety and are therefore more interesting.

The point is that one way to freshen up an activity, a program, or a service is to offer it in collaboration with some other organization. It likely will be a better use of community resources and it very well may turn out that more people attend the program or utilize the service.

Chapter 20

Community: Awareness and Collaboration

So far we have been asking you to think about and take some leadership for your board and for your organization. Now we ask you to consider your community. You do wear a community citizen hat in addition to the one you wear as a board member. And while all these pages have been directed at you wearing your board hat, we would like to ask you to look more broadly. Both you and your organization, after all, exist in a broader community of people and organizations. It is about that greater good that we now ask you to think. In doing so we acknowledge this is all far closer to philosophy than practicality, but then effective board leadership surely encompasses both. So stick with us here and you just may wish to try this conversation with your executive and the rest of the board.

A LITTLE PHILOSOPHY

An organization can be mission-faithful and ethically clean, and at the same time altogether too absorbed in its own life. For human beings in infancy and severe personal trauma, self-absorption is necessary, even acceptable. Likewise, fresh new organizations and those in serious crisis understandably are self-absorbed and altogether internally focused. As an ongoing way of being, however, organizational self-absorption is less than healthy and would not rate high in most systems of ethics.

What does this mean for your organization? At the least, it means that one of the challenges facing you is making a near constant reference to the place and role of your organization in the overall scheme of things. It means doing what you do as an organization with integrity and excellence but also considering the impact of your action on the life of the broader community. It means continuously balancing organizational mission and priorities with the needs and priorities of the larger community of organizations. Perhaps most radically, it means a kind of organizational selflessness versus self-absorption.

Here are some examples. One organization refused to pursue a grant from a community foundation because in that moment of history a smaller colleague organization needed it more. Another organization decided not to initiate a new program direction because it would have constituted unfair (meaning more prestigious and powerful) competition with a smaller, more single-focused agency. Yet another urged a particularly effective board member to take a leave of absence and serve on the board of a colleague organization struggling through a painful personnel problem. Wouldn't it be nice if organizational selflessness grew to be as common and newsworthy as often-reported accounts of personal selflessness?

For what, after all, is the goal of not-for-profit organizations? While there are not shareholders, there is a balance sheet important to keep out of the red. But that probably is not the most important bottom line. We propose a notion that may contribute to balance, perspective, and sanity. From for-profits we have learned the importance of focus and market niche. Perhaps what we give back for the good of the community is peripheral vision. Market niche can degenerate to singleness of purpose and then to organizational isolation and self-absorption. Peripheral vision is not merely fixing your gaze on your own balance sheet, but paying attention to the fortunes of others. It is the attitude of the common good under which, and by which, you ultimately judge all your organizational efforts. Organizational selflessness renounces competition in favor of connectedness. It pays close attention to the well-being of other community groups and institutions. The concept of peripheral vision goes beyond seeing broadly to acting broadly for others.

We cannot imagine what that might be like in your own organizational situation. We can imagine, with the press of your own agency agendas, that the concept of organizational selflessness has yet to emerge. Our experience is that some not-for-profit organizations operate quite continually with the self-image of sacrifice: the salaries are low, the clients are predominantly underprivileged, and the measurable successes are few. And it is many of those same conditions that keep us self-focused and force us to work against a wider vision and a healthier community.

Earlier, we challenged you to think of your board participation as a partnership not merely with your board and executive, and we now challenge you to think of your organization's life in broad partnerships beyond the well-being of your own particular mission. We ourselves hope for a connectedness in serving and a willingness to modify pure organizational interest for the good of the broader community. Carrying those values into the rich and diverse community of organizations that exist in any area may be the special gift that the not-for-profit world gives to all citizens.

A WORD ABOUT COLLABORATION

There are at least two public perceptions about not-for-profit organizations that would be useful for you to counteract. One is that there are just too many such organizations that do essentially the same thing. The second is that they are very territorial and not inclined to cooperate with one another. No one knows what the optimum number of not-for-profit organizations of one kind or another really is, any more than what the optimum number of drug stores or gas stations is. We do know that it is healthy for not-for-profit organizations to have a spirit of cooperation and, in a self-interested way, that cooperation is likely to increase their base of clients or the size of their audiences. For whatever mix of reasons, we encourage you to be a board member who is always asking, "Is there someone else in town we should talk to about doing this new proposal jointly?" or "Is there anyone who already does after school programs or midweek concerts or Saturday schools with whom we could partner?"

True collaborations—partnerships in something old or new— are not easy and the costs need to be carefully measured. Costs in this case are not merely money but staff, volunteer time, and the energy required to meld two organizations' different ways of doing something into one better way. As citizens of the community, board members need to take the lead in asking about and acting on collaboration in a way that models openness and a sense of the big picture.

In practicing collaboration, we suggest you first try collaborating on a single event or project. This is good practice, because you will get to see what all the issues are. After smoothing out the rough spots (since there will always be things to work on), consider a year-long trial on Program X. Whether Program X is an after school activity or a series of summer performances in the park, the point is to try out the new partnership first. Then you can sit down and evaluate, change, and with luck repeat the next year.

The final and most complete form of collaboration is a merger. You may have experienced the challenges of it with a small church or small business. It can be tough and it can be terrific. Many times it brings more and better resources to those you wish to serve. Mergers can also save money, and there is often a way to build an ongoing identity and respect for the history and specialness of each organization. Many find that mergers are most easily accomplished when one of the two merging organizations is without an executive director. In either case, a committee from each board needs to take the lead. What follows are some questions to think through before a merger, or even a long-term collaboration.

1. Why would we do this?
2. What are the advantages and disadvantages for those we serve, our programs or our organizations?
3. Is the timing good now or would it be better in six months or a year from now?
4. What is likely to happen if we don't do this?
5. What are the forces in the community urging us to do this or not to do this? Do we care?
6. How can we do this and still honor our own history and maintain some identity?
7. Can we do this in stages? For example, can we maintain our own office locations for a year until we find a new place for both parties?
8. Who do we know that has been through this and can advise us?
9. Can we do this for a specified period of time (two to three years) and then review and amend the agreement?
10. How will we know this has been successful?

In short, we think you should put your community hat on and try cooperating with another organization on a project, then perhaps collaborating on that program on an ongoing basis. By then it may make sense to ask the merger questions.

Chapter 21

Friendly Marketing: Listening and Speaking

Some people may be surprised to learn that marketing is both speaking and listening. It is telling the story about who you are as an organization and what you do, and it is telling that story in response to what the community tells you is most needed. Marketing is an entirely good and right thing for you to do as a not-for-profit organization. The friendly marketing that we suggest you do does not exaggerate the truth ("take this miracle pill and lose 40 pounds in two weeks") nor does it pressure or twist arms ("your house is probably full of thousands of invisible and dangerous dust mites").

You probably do not need to become a marketing expert or even hire a high-priced one. There are some things to think about and do as you try to listen to your community and find the best way to tell your story and provide your services. What follows is an outline of suggestions from our own experience.

First there are some definitions that need to be explained. If we were to ask you what the first thing is that comes to mind when you hear the word marketing, our guess is that you would say advertising. Most people do. Unfortunately, that is only a small part of it and comes under the heading of promotion. Writing an ad for the local weekly news is not unimportant but it is not the challenging and creative part of marketing. The best of marketing is driven more by thinking than doing. We'd like to give you five things to think about as part of your marketing effort. Remember that they are, taken together, what marketing is all about, and only one of them is promoting through advertising.

1. Design the activity.

If what it is that you are offering does not make sense, is needed by almost no one, or is already being offered by two other agencies in your town, now is the time to stop. No amount of ads or shouting about it on T.V. or radio will make much of a difference. You start with need and design a program in response to that need. This is why it is so very important to have the people who know about the substance of the program or service in the same room and in the same conversation with the people who know the most about the people in the community. That is where and with whom the designing should take place. It is in that creative, sometimes stressful place between artists and marketing specialists, between social work counselors and those most familiar with the citizens, that the best and most useful designing can take place.

Designing the activity may or may not take surveys, and may or may not call for focus groups. You do not have to do only or exactly what people say. But if after surveys and talking you can find no one who likes the idea of brass bands on Monday night or group therapy Tuesday noon, you probably need to rethink it. So, as a starting place, as a first marketing step, check the needs and design your service or program with those needs strongly in mind.

2. Planning

This is not the big organization-wide planning that we talked about in Chapter 7. This is specific decision-making about the specific program that you have designed, knowing what is most needed in your community. It is the second step in marketing and it too is a thinking step far more than a doing step.

For example, you now know because you asked and people told you that a parenthood training group would be well received on Sunday afternoons. That is the beginning of a plan. You have the day and time of day. But many additional questions need to be thoughtfully considered and answered if you are to complete your marketing plan. They include:

- How many sessions?
- How long for each?
- How will people find out about this?
- Where will it be held?
- Is there an obvious partner?
- Is this only for first-time parents?
- Will young children be permitted to attend or will there be child care?
- What will it cost?
- Will there be scholarship support?
- What are the credentials of those offering the training?
- And ...?

Again, the point here is that those who know about parent effectiveness training and those who best know the community need to make the plan together. If only the marketing people make it, the danger is that there will be a lack of substance and comprehensiveness. If only the trainers design it the danger is that it will be planned for places, times of day, fees, and lengths of time that will not work for the people in this particular community. Joint planning is step two—another thinking step.

3. Pricing

It is very hard to generalize on this one. There are so many different community financial situations and so many different activities. However, this is another case where if you do not make a good decision, no matter how good the program is and no matter how many ways you talk about it, it will not work. One generality is that no matter what the price is, discounts and/or scholarships need to be available. The amount well-employed people can and should pay is probably different than what seniors on social security, students, and those whose kids are on the free lunch program should pay.

Comparing what you plan to charge with what other successful programs are charging for similar activities is an obvious starting place. You should always strive to strike a balance between too high a price, which keeps many people from attending, and too low, which causes some to think it isn't worth much.

4. Promotion

Finally here comes the action step. Now that you have designed, planned, and priced, you are ready to promote. Depending on your budget, you may or may not be able to purchase ads, print posters, mail flyers, or do anything else that costs very much. Consider, though, that a carefully organized word of mouth campaign, well-placed public service announcements (that means they are free) on T.V. or radio, or newsy pictures and articles in your local paper can be just as effective. You will have to decide what works best for your community and of course what is workable with your budget.

5. Gathering feedback

This final step is too often overlooked as part of a marketing plan. Recall that in the first step, designing the activity, we talked about identifying needs and listening to your community. We end as well with listening. This listening, however, is mostly with those who attended your event or utilized your service. It is from them that you want to know how you can do better. You may want to get some of that feedback in writing with audience response forms. Make sure these forms are not too lengthy or solicited too often or you'll drive the audience away. After all, they did come for education or entertainment, not to join a focus group. You may want to design a sample for people to fill out after they have completed their training program or counseling sessions.

Conversation is also good. Ask people how it went. Encourage them to make suggestions about how it could be better. If you communicate that what you always wish to do as an organization is to keep improving, audience members will be less likely to offer comments that seem only like criticism, and more likely to help you with suggestions.

Whether in writing or in person, the gathering thoughtful responses step is valuable in adjusting not only what the service or program is but where, when, and how it is offered. We find that a very simple form with open-ended questions is both useful and easy to fill out. Here's a sample.

1. I will tell at least one person that the best thing about this program is _____.

2. I would have liked this program even better if _____ _____.

3. If I could change one thing to make this a better program, it would be _____.

4. I think this program could be even better if there was more of _____ and less of _____.

5. Another suggestion I would make is _____.

You may wish to design a more formal rating sheet with several categories and numerical ratings. That too can work. Remember to keep a balance between what will be genuinely useful to the organization and what is not too much to ask of a participant.

In short, start with listening, end with listening, and do a thoughtful job of planning, pricing, and promotion and you should come up with a good marketing plan. Most importantly, your marketing will feel friendly, which is probably at least one of the important feelings you would like people to have about your organization.

C h a p t e r 2 2

Trustworthy: Thinking about Ethical Decisions

A s a board member, you are officially a trustee of your organization. You are entrusted with the mission and life of the organization. In addition, the government, by granting you special not-for-profit tax-exempt status, entrusts you with that responsibility, and the community must also believe you to be worthy of trust. More often than not, you and the board members that serve on not-for-profit boards in your community are entirely trustworthy. However, from time to time, real problems sneak up on and surprise us. We are trying to do the work of the board and, all of a sudden, something unforeseen happens.

Too often, paying the necessary attention to matters urgent and pressing produces a numbness to ethical matters. Boards find themselves blindsided by ethical problems that may seem obvious afterward, but in the practical push of daily activity are overlooked. What follows is a list of often-encountered ethical issues that we hope serves as a forewarning. These issues appear just about everywhere and no doubt will eventually end up in your very own organizational lap. Consider them now so that you can minimize surprises and decide in advance policy positions on what, for most, are common ethical issues.

Review the issues and examples of each as a full board. Some of the items may seem obvious and self-evident; others are likely to cause discussion. There may be two or three worth addressing in a way that will result in a policy statement for your board. In the course of it all, you may stumble onto an additional two or three that are particularly critical in your organizational situation. Our intent is not that you develop a comprehensive code of ethics but that you become more aware of the ethical issues most likely to impose themselves on your organization and prepare in advance to address what otherwise could be surprising impositions.

1. Fidelity to mission

What are the decisions and/or actions most likely to pull the organization in a direction counter to its mission?

Examples:

- Accepting funds with restrictive purposes or expectations
- Attempting to be all things to all people
- Bowing to political interests of board members and employees that are beyond the mission of the organization

2. Respect for individuals

What are the desired standards for the organization's treatment of board members, staff, and constituents?

Examples:

- Defining compensation levels appropriate to the nature of the organization
- Developing employee policies and practices that are reflective of or in harmony with the mission
- Setting traditions for the way in which volunteers are selected, managed, and recognized

3. Inclusion and exclusivity

When is it appropriate in the organization for a person or group to make significant unilateral decisions affecting others?

Examples:

- Determining who should be sought out for advice and consultation on significant decisions
- Deciding if some decisions require more than a majority vote
- Considering if the board is reflective of the constituency
- Considering the influence of committees and organizational structure
- Considering who may attend specific committee meetings

4. Openness and secrecy

What, if anything, should be kept secret or in confidence, and from whom and why?

Examples:

- Financial information and level of detail
- Personnel data and files
- Donor information
- Proceedings of specific committees
- Real estate transactions
- Contract information and bidding

5. Conflict of interest

Are there ways in which we function that result in inappropriate benefit to board members, staff, or constituents?

Examples:

- Undue constituent influence
- Undue financial benefit of board members
- Unfair contracting practices involving directors or friends
- Personal or intimate relationships within the organization

6. Stewardship and finance

What should the not-for-profit organization do to assure that expenditures and resources reflect its present mission and long-term health?

Examples:

- Resource allocation (how available funds are to be expended)
- Investment of funds/resources in ways inappropriate to the mission
- Spending for the present without regard for meeting the mission in years to come

7. Personal integrity

What are the personal standards the organization wishes to encourage with respect to honesty and respect for people and property?

Examples:

- Keeping confidential information confidential (donor records, client data, personnel files)
- Honoring commitments (signed and unsigned)
- Considering whether the organization's board and employees are trusted to tell the truth
- Establishing integrity with finances as a priority
- Presenting financial reports to the public in a straightforward manner

8. Political integrity

What are the guidelines the organization wishes to use for participation in advocacy, fundraising, and interaction with other organizations?

Examples:

- Determining how information/data for advocacy purposes will be interpreted
- Setting a policy or tradition that discourages undue pressure being placed on prospects for contributions or grants
- Deciding what, if any, mutually beneficial arrangements should be encouraged
- Setting expectations which discourage the manipulation of volunteers to gain desired results

The above list represents only a number of potential areas for concern. While you may identify other potential ethical issues for your organization, these should demonstrate the general range of issues and the challenge of maintaining authentic behavior.

Your response to the checklist

Rare is the organization that needs to deal with all of the above issues. You can play an important role in developing a list of ethical concerns that you believe are most closely related to your own organization.

Once an initial list has been created, the board can discuss which issues are relevant and, of course, consider additional issues. Once the critical issues have been established, the board can develop appropriate policy responses for each one that is a concern.

Reviewing organizational behavior with an eye to the ethical consequences of the stated mission can be an invigorating experience for the board. This approach can be taken with budgeting, programming, personnel policy, and numerous other aspects of the organization's life. Thus, a simple proposal can take on a new dimension when examined for its impact on and faithfulness to the organization's mission.

For example, many have observed the havoc caused by undue constituent influence or an exclusive approach to solving community challenges. While it may not be the intent, groups often hear only the viewpoints of those in their inner circle. For these reasons, groups become weakened in their ability to incorporate new ideas, deal with change, and reflect all relevant viewpoints.

Money and power can interfere with a not-for-profit organization's mission and vision. Major donors, due to the size of their contributions and their ties to an organization's board, may try to exercise undue influence. Indeed, they can become the tail wagging the dog. An observed policy on conflict of interest or exclusive behavior can significantly enhance the board's ability to deal with such challenging situations.

Ethical challenges are not always readily apparent and often come about when least expected. The board best serves by keeping the organization in touch with its mission and vigilant for ethical problems that could deter or derail adherence to that mission.

Chapter 23

Celebrations

You may remember that we started out this small book talking about satisfactions—more satisfying lives for those we serve and more personally satisfying ways for us to participate in this good work. If our first word is satisfaction, our last but not least word is celebrations. Most of us know and remember big celebrations when an agency turned twenty-five or an executive had served for ten years or when a mortgage was burned. Those are important milestones in the life of an organization and when they do occur, they are usually celebrated well. Now, however, we want to ask you to think about a different kind of celebration that does not necessarily take planning, money, or a fancy invitation.

Here's why: the work we do as not-for-profit organizations is often hard. Board members and staff put in long hours to do that work well and get it done on time. And it doesn't seem to stop—there are fewer and fewer off seasons or even off hours. You finish one newsletter and it's time for big event planning. You finish one big event and it is time to do the budget, write a proposal, or get out a huge mailing. That just may be unavoidable given the way life seems to be lived these days at work, at home, and in volunteer work. What we suggest here is to pause in the middle of the craziness and stress of organizational life and take the time to celebrate.

Maybe calling this a celebration is too much—too grand. For it can be as simple as a three-minute pause in a board meeting or a staff meeting, or just spontaneously after something really great has happened ("we just got our first grant from the community foundation") or something really big is completed ("we just finished organizing all the papers, photos, and clippings since we started out in 1978"). You don't need punch, cookies, and flowers, although any one of those would be just fine. What you do need is quiet time and simple words of joy and appreciation. If that time is not taken, you immediately race on to the next big challenge without celebrating the happy conclusion of the one just passed.

Perhaps you could have some fun with it and appoint a particularly thoughtful board or staff member as "the officer in charge of small celebrations." This individual would have the right to break in on any serious committee or board meeting with a small "time-out" to savor a success and to thank the few people who made it happen. After all, we usually don't wolf down a perfectly done steak in five minutes or speed-read a lovely poem. Neither should we race from task to task in organizations without pausing now and again to reflect on a good thing done or a big project finished. Try it. We think it will make organizational life more pleasant. We write about it here with such vigor because we know that we ourselves need to be reminded to have those small celebrations that so enrich our work and life together in these dear and good organizations.

Speaking of celebrations, if you have arrived here at the end on page 136, congratulations. Thanks for sticking with us on these pages and participating in these conversations about board membership. We are glad there are people like you who care enough to try to do an effective job of being a board member. Our only regret is not being able to sit and talk with each of you. Do drop us a note about your work, your satisfactions and celebrations, and of course let us know how we can make another edition of this book more helpful and even better. After all, this doing of a good thing yet better is what these pages are all about.

Afterwords

We have traveled on these pages from satisfactions to celebrations and covered a lot of territory in between. The six of us have tried to imagine your life as a board member and keep you in mind as we wrote. We all agree it would have been much nicer to sit down with you, hear about your work, and respond in person. We do want to let you know that we took at least two pieces of advice that we have written about and applied them to ourselves. First, we have insisted on having some good fun and personal satisfaction in preparing these pages. It has been satisfying to us and will be even more so if it proves to be genuinely useful to you.

Secondly, we celebrated. We had a publication reception on November 7, 2002 at Edison Community College in Piqua, Ohio. We made a gift of this small book to all the board members in attendance from Darke, Miami, and Shelby Counties. We did all the formal thank-you's and had very good refreshments. Each of us then said a personal word about the experience of writing this book and what was most important about it. In closing, here are some of these words from each of us to each of you.

"Successful not-for-profit boards result from combining dedicated, competent board members with effective, efficient processes. If you can achieve both components as you serve, you will receive the satisfaction of serving well."

— Richard Adams

✧

"Working on this book was a reflective journey highlighting the commitment that you make to the organization when accepting the invitation to become a board member. Be true to your beliefs and do not overextend yourself to the point that you cannot fully participate in the decisions and activities that you promised to devote to the organization."

— Shirley Magoteaux

"Keep in mind that everything you do should enrich your life as well as enrich your community. I believe it is important that as you help to energize the quality of not-for-profit organizations, and also motivate others to do so, that you feel rewarded too."
— Virginia Matz

"As you consider your participation on a board I encourage you to be passionate about the organization and its mission You have the power to do awesome things in your community and to truly make a difference in the lives of people. What a great opportunity! Seize the moment."
— Cheryl Stiefel-Francis

"Attendance! Just like back in grade school, perfect attendance will be rewarded. You'll never miss anything going on with your organization, and with this involvement, your commitment to the mission will grow."
— Judy Westerheide

So many organizations in so many counties in our nation depend upon thoughtful and committed people like you. We are grateful for all the ways you have found to help.

Other Suggested Reading

De Pree, M. (2001). *Called to serve: Creating and nurturing the effective volunteer board*. Grand Rapids, Michigan: Eerdmans Publishing Company.

Houle, C.O. (1989) *Governing boards: their nature and nurture*. San Francisco: Jossey-Bass.

Leifer, J.C. & Glomb, M.B. (1993). *The legal obligations of nonprofit boards*. Washington, D.C.: National Center for Nonprofit Boards.

O'Connell, B. (1993) *The board member's book: making a difference in voluntary organizations*. New York: Foundation Center.

O'Connell, B. (1988). *The role of the board and board members*. Washington, D.C.: Independent Sector.

Panas, J. (1991). *Boardroom verities: A celebration of trusteeship with some guides and techniques to govern*. Chicago: Precept Press.

Robinson, M.K. (2001). *Nonprofit boards that work: The end of one-size-fits all governance*. New York: John Wiley & Sons.

Rutledge, J.M. (1994). *Building board diversity*. Washington, D.C.: National Center for Nonprofit Boards.

Scott, K.T. (2000). *Creating caring and capable boards: Reclaiming the passion for active trusteeship*. San Francisco: Jossey-Bass.

Szanton, P. (1992). *Board assessment of the organization: How are we doing?* Washington, D.C.: National Center for Nonprofit Boards.

Vickers, D.F. et.al. (2000). *The president's book: Experiencing the essentials with six board presidents*. Columbus, Ohio: The Academy for Leadership and Governance.

Zeitlin, K.A. & Dorn, S.E. (1996). *The nonprofit board's guide to bylaws*. Washington, D.C.: National Center for Nonprofit Boards.